A GANNETT COMPANY

# Lifeline

## BIOGRAPHIES

# Jay-Z

## CEO of Hip-Hop

by **Stephen G. Gordon**

Twenty-First Century Books · Minneapolis

*To Jackie, who sat under my desk while I wrote this one.*

Twenty-First Century Books
A division of Lerner Publishing Group, Inc.
241 First Avenue North
Minneapolis, MN 55401 U.S.A.

Website address: www.lernerbooks.com


Library of Congress Cataloging-in-Publication Data

Gordon, Stephen G.
    Jay-Z : CEO of hip-hop / by Stephen G. Gordon.
        p. cm. — (USA today lifeline biographies)
    Includes bibliographical references and index.
    ISBN 978-1-4677-0811-1 (lib. bdg. : alk. paper)
    1. Jay-Z, 1969– —Juvenile literature. 2. Rap musicians—United States—Biography—
Juvenile literature. I. Title.
ML3930.J38G67  2013
782.421649092—dc23 [B]                                        2012020993

Manufactured in the United States of America
1 – CG – 12/31/12

![USA TODAY — A GANNETT COMPANY] Lifeline
BIOGRAPHIES

www.usatoday.com

USA TODAY
A GANNETT COMPANY

**Award winner:** Jay-Z (Shawn Carter) shows off his threads (and a Grammy Award) at the 2006 Grammys.

# Do It Yourself

Shawn Carter had talent—a lot of talent. Even as a teenager, he showed a special gift for rapping. When he picked up a mic, rhymes flowed effortlessly from his tongue. He rapped about growing up in poverty. He rapped about drug dealing. He rapped about violence. These were topics Shawn knew well.

Shawn had grown up during the 1970s and the 1980s in the Marcy Houses, a housing development in New York City.

Marcy was home to more than four thousand residents—most of them black and all of them poor. Amid the poverty, Shawn found a way to make money. At the age of fifteen, he started selling crack cocaine, an addictive, illegal drug. Dealing drugs thrust Shawn into a world filled with guns and gangs.

At the same time Shawn traded in addiction and ugliness, he also created something beautiful. He made up poetic raps and performed them anywhere he could find an audience: in clubs, on local radio shows, and on the sidewalks outside the Marcy Houses. He took the stage name Jay-Z.

By the time he had reached his twenties, Jay-Z wanted to take his art to the next level. He wanted to leave drug dealing behind and make music full-time. Damon Dash, who managed hip-hop artists, tried to land a record deal for Jay-Z. But every record label Dash and Jay-Z talked to—Columbia, Def Jam, and others—turned them down.

Jay-Z was disappointed, but he also saw an opportunity. If he couldn't get a record label to sign him, then the solution was simple: he would start his own record company. That way, he could call his own shots and determine his own future. He wouldn't have to answer to any record company executives. He would be the executive.

Jay-Z, Dash, and another friend, Kareem "Biggs" Burke, put their heads and their money together. They drew up a business plan and founded a company: Roc-A-Fella Records. The three men dreamed big, but they started small. First, Jay-Z recorded a single, "I Can't Get with That," in a basement studio. A filmmaker friend shot a low-budget video to go with the record. Then the Roc-A-Fella team hustled the song in person to DJs, record stores, and radio stations.

Fast-forward to the present. Jay-Z, the former drug dealer, has become one of the biggest names in hip-hop. He has sold more than 50 million albums and won nine Grammy Awards. He is a business mogul, with wealth estimated at more than $450 million. He's friendly with princes and presidents. Jay-Z's rise in the music industry is a tale of determination and inspiration, and a true rags-to-riches story.

**Smile:** Shawn Carter (*middle*) sits for a middle school class photo. He attended school in Brooklyn, New York.

# Child's Play

On December 4, 1969, Adnis "A. J." Reeves and Gloria Carter welcomed a new baby into their family. They named him Shawn Corey Carter. Baby Shawn had two big sisters, Michelle (known as Mickey) and Andrea (called Annie), and a big brother, Eric.

The family lived in Brooklyn, a borough of New York City, in a house on Lexington Avenue. A.J.'s parents, Ruby Reeves and Adnis Reeves Sr., owned the house. They lived there too. Shawn later remembered sitting on the front stoop of the house, "just chillin'" on summer evenings.

When Shawn was about four, his uncle gave him an old ten-speed bike. The bike was too big for Shawn, so instead of sitting on the bike's seat, he slid one leg underneath the bar that connected the seat to the handlebars. In this awkward position, he pedaled up and down Lexington Avenue. His neighbors cheered him on. Shawn later said that showing off on the bike gave him his first taste of fame. He liked the feeling.

When Shawn was five, the family left his grandparents' house. They moved a few blocks away to the Marcy Houses, a big housing development for low-income families. More than four thousand residents lived in apartments in the six-story buildings. Shawn's family lived in apartment 5C. Shawn and Eric shared a room there.

Shawn attended P.S. (public school) 168, an elementary school in Brooklyn. He loved playing sports in the afternoon. He joined a Little

**Family bond:** Shawn puts his arms around his mother *(right)* and grandmother *(left)* in 2001. He grew up in a close-knit family.

**Super fly:** Shawn Carter grew up listening to the music of R & B great Curtis Mayfield, pictured here in 1973.

**Dig it:** The legendary composer Isaac Hayes, pictured here in 1995, gained fame with albums such as *Hot Buttered Soul*.

League baseball team. He and his friends shot hoops on neighborhood playgrounds and played football in a nearby field. The boys had to be careful when they played football. The field they played in was littered with broken glass. It could cut right through their tennis shoes and into their feet.

## Sound Track

Shawn's parents were crazy about music. They loved R & B (rhythm and blues) artists such as the Commodores, Curtis Mayfield, Stevie Wonder, the Four Tops, Isaac Hayes, Marvin Gaye, the Temptations, and the Jackson 5. A.J. and Gloria kept hundreds of LPs (long-playing records) in metal milk crates in their apartment. The crates were stacked one on top of another, all the way to the ceiling. "My house was the house around the neighborhood that everybody went to because we had all the newest records, and we just had super cool parents," Jay-Z remembered later. "Music filled the house with emotion and joy and feeling."

Every Saturday night, the whole family watched *Soul Train*. This TV show was a showcase for soul and R & B musicians. The show's smooth host Don Cornelius introduced viewers to new talents. Watching the performances on TV, Shawn, his sisters, and his cousin B-High danced around the living room. Shawn pretended to be the lead singer while his sisters sang backup.

When Shawn was nine, the hip-hop crew the Sugarhill Gang performed on *Soul Train*. Shawn was thrilled to see rappers on TV.

**Rap originals:** Shawn's life changed when he heard "Rapper's Delight," a song by the hip-hop group the Sugarhill Gang, pictured here in 1980.

**February 2, 2012**

# *Soul Train* laid the rails of a cultural revolution

<u>From the Pages of</u>
<u>USA TODAY</u>

Armed with sharp suits and a mesmerizing voice, Don Cornelius set out in 1970 to entertain viewers of Chicago's WCIU with a song-and-dance TV show called *Soul Train*. Turns out, America wanted in on the party.

Cornelius, 75, died Wednesday at his home in Sherman Oaks, California. The music maverick struck financial and cultural gold with *Soul Train*, whose 35 years on the air made it the longest first-run syndicated show in history, with an effect that crossed generations and races.

"*Soul Train* gave the black community reason to be proud," says Kenneth Gamble, half of the fabled songwriting team Gamble & Huff, who wrote the show's chugging theme song, known as T.S.O.P (The Sound of Philadelphia). "It was so rare at the time to see someone black doing anything like that."

If Dick Clark's *American Bandstand* was Saturday morning's placid place to play, *Soul Train*, with its driving music and innovative dancers, was the coolest party you could hope to crash. "That show was the centerpiece of my Saturdays," says hip-hop artist Terius "The-Dream" Nash, who performed on the program in 2005.

*Soul Train* "had a substantial impact and was very much a part of contemporary music history," says Clive Davis, the record mogul who nurtured the careers of Aretha Franklin, Whitney Houston and Dionne Warwick. "His show reached a sizable and devoted audience, and every major artist of the time did it and did it willingly."

With his smooth, resonant baritone, Cornelius introduced hundreds of stars to the nation's multicultural TV audience, including James Brown, Jerry Butler, Marvin Gaye, the O'Jays and Barry White. In the background was a colorful menagerie of partiers who influenced dance and fashion and opened a window onto black culture that had received scant media exposure.

*Soul Train*'s role in pushing black culture into the mainstream cannot be underestimated, says Mark Anthony Neal, professor of black popular culture at Duke

University. "Motown had laid down the sonic groundwork, but Don Cornelius let you visualize it," he says. "Black power was visible on *Soul Train*."

The program was rife with iconic elements. There was the Soul Train line, in which pairs of dancers popped creative dance moves and flashed outrageous jumpsuits and Afros on their way down. The Scramble Board gave two dancers 60 seconds to unscramble the name of a notable African-American entertainer or historical figure. The dancers became stars in their own right and created moves such as locking, roboting and waacking (later known as voguing) that would be replicated at clubs and parties around the world.

**Soul man:** Don Cornelius, pictured here in 2005, was the longtime host of TV's *Soul Train*. The program was a showcase for notable acts in R & B and, later, hip-hop.

"He was the host with the most," says Jermaine Hall, editor of *Vibe* magazine. "He was the representation of cool. He put across to the culture at large what was going on in the African-American community, much the way, later on, hip-hop would do the same."

—Marco R. della Cava and Steve Jones

Another name for a rapper is an emcee. The name comes from the initials *MC*, which stand for "master of ceremonies."

**Old school:** In the 1980s, the trio Run-D.M.C. from New York helped take hip-hop to the mainstream with hits such as "It's Tricky."

On a song called "Rapper's Delight," the Sugarhill Gang's three emcees took turns reciting rhymes into the microphone while a heavy beat played behind them. The year was 1979, and hip-hop was new on the music scene. "Rappers Delight" was the first hip-hop song to become a hit.

In the decade that followed, hip-hop exploded across the nation. Rapper Kurtis Blow, the group Run-D.M.C., and the DJ Grandmaster Flash released hit records. Hip-hop was huge in big inner-city neighborhoods. In the Marcy Houses, teenagers strolled around with big boom boxes on their shoulders, blasting hip-hop from the speakers. People drove through Marcy with beats booming from their car radios.

## "I Could *Do* That"

For Shawn and other kids in Marcy, hip-hop wasn't just something you listened to. It was something you could do yourself. Anyone could make up raps. You didn't need any instruments or equipment.

One day when Shawn was nine, he saw a group of Marcy kids standing in a circle. Inside the circle, a boy named Slate was rapping. The kids who surrounded him clapped their hands to provide a beat. Slate "was rhyming, throwing out couplet [two-line verse] after couplet like he was in a trance . . . straight off the top of his head, never losing the beat, riding the handclaps," Shawn remembered later.

Shawn was dazzled by Slate's performance. As he watched, he thought to himself, "I could *do* that." That very night, he started writing his own rhymes. He scribbled them down in a spiral notebook.

After that, Shawn rapped all the time. He pounded out beats on the kitchen table and practiced his raps around the house. Shawn's mom gave him a three-ring binder filled with unlined paper. He filled every square inch with rhymes. "Almost obsessively, I would write and write," he once said.

He carried the binder with him when he hung out with his friends. Whenever a rap came to mind, he wrote it in the binder. If he didn't have his binder, he wrote the lyrics on a paper bag or just memorized them. He said, "I would just have four or five songs that I hadn't written down in my mind."

## Best and Brightest

Shawn didn't read many books at home. At school, he was often bored. He daydreamed about being a famous rapper or a baseball or basketball star. But he was nevertheless a good student. He excelled at English and liked looking up new words in the dictionary. He could do math problems in his head.

# IN FOCUS

## Hip-Hop History

Hip-hop music features spoken rhymes—raps—over instrumental music. According to *Jet* magazine, the term *hip-hop* originated with Keith "Cowboy" Wiggins. Wiggins was a rapper in the hip-hop crew the Furious Five. In 1978 Wiggins was teasing a friend who had just joined the army. Wiggins sang "hip hop, hip hop" to his friend, imitating the chants recited by soldiers as they marched. Later, Wiggins used the "hip hop" chant in his stage shows. In 1979 the Sugarhill Gang included the phrase "hip-hop" in its song "Rapper's Delight." By 1981 DJs were referring to rap music as hip-hop.

**Cowboy and crew:** Grandmaster Flash and the Furious Five pose in 1986. Keith Wiggins (*center, wearing white*) might be the person who gave hip-hop its name.

"I knew I was witty around the sixth grade," he said later. "I just had that feeling of being smart." Teachers gave him a series of tests, which revealed that sixth-grader Shawn was performing at a twelfth-grade level. "I was crazy happy about that," Shawn remembered. He was proud of his smarts and especially proud of his raps. "Even back then, I thought I was the best."

www.usatoday.com

USA TODAY
A GANNETT COMPANY

**CHAPTER TWO**

SUPERJET
2ⁿᵈ FLOOR OFFICES FOR RENT
CALL 265-5570
SEA · AIR · T
FARM GAMES
LOVES HOME
PIT FUN
SIGNAL
24 HRS
FREE PARKING

**Times Square:** New York City's Times Square area, seen here in the mid-1970s, is one of the city's busiest places. Shawn Carter used to visit Times Square with his father.

# Trouble

Shawn loved his father. A. J. Reeves taught Shawn how to play chess and basketball. He introduced Shawn to classic R & B music. Sometimes A. J. took Shawn and B-High to Times Square, a bustling intersection in the borough of Manhattan. They'd hang out, watch all the colorful people on the streets, and then eat steaks and french fries at Lindy's, a famous New York restaurant.

When Shawn was about eleven, his happy times with his father ended. A. J.'s little brother, Shawn's uncle Ray, was murdered outside a Brooklyn bar. The police did not find or arrest the killer. A. J. became obsessed with tracking down the killer himself. His grief led him to drink heavily and later to use drugs. His life spiraled downward. He left the family, moving back to his parents' house. He and Shawn's mother, Gloria, divorced.

Gloria was left alone to raise four children. She worked as a clerk at an investment company and took additional jobs as necessary to pay the bills.

## Jaz-O and Jay-Z

Shawn's outlook darkened after his father left. He withdrew from his mother. Although he was highly intelligent, he did poorly at school. "My dad was such a good dad that when he left, he left a huge scar," Jay-Z remarked later. "He was my superhero." One of Jay-Z's few positive outlets was rapping. He was able to pour out his feelings into rhymes.

In 1984 Shawn met a rapper named Jonathan "Jaz-O" Burks. Four years older than Shawn, Jaz-O also lived in the Marcy Houses. Shawn's talent immediately impressed the older boy. "When he rhymed, I heard something I'd never heard before," Jaz-O remembered later.

**Mentor:** Jonathan "Jaz-O" Burks drops by a party in 2005. Jaz-O helped Jay-Z enter the world of hip-hop.

# IN FOCUS

## Don't Forget

Jay-Z says he has a photographic memory. In a 2000 interview, he explained, "When I'd be out on the street [hustling], I couldn't write down lyrics, so I had to hold things longer in my head. And the longer I started holding the lyrics, the more I got used to it. I was holding 16 bars [lines of music] one day, then a whole song, then two songs. It just became something natural and normal for me to do." Later, while making albums, Jay-Z rarely wrote down lyrics. He made them up in his head, rehearsed them a few times, and recited them in the recording studio.

"The cadence [rhythm], the things that people may have as far as raw talent . . . he had it."

Jaz-O became a mentor to Shawn. He taught Shawn how to sharpen his delivery when he rapped. He taught him to weave metaphors (symbols) and clever wordplay into his lyrics. Shawn's mom gave him a boom box with a mic. He and Jaz began to put their raps on tape. They played the rhymes back and figured out how to improve them.

Like every good rapper, Shawn needed a stage name. His childhood nickname was Jazzy, and that name morphed into the name Jay-Z. The name had special meaning because it was similar to Jaz-O. It also referenced the J and Z subway lines that stopped near the Marcy Houses.

Jay-Z, Jaz-O, and the other rappers in Marcy didn't need a stage to show off their talents. They simply rapped on sidewalks and in the hallways at school. Boys often held contests, called battles, to determine the best rapper. Surrounded by a cipher, or circle of listeners, each rapper took his turn. He freestyled, or made up rhymes off the top of his head. He bragged about himself and also insulted and teased his opponent. The rapper who got the loudest cheers and applause from the audience was the winner.

"There were some real talents in Marcy," Jay-Z recalled in his book *Decoded*. "DJs started setting up sound systems in the . . . courtyards, and me and Jaz and other MCs [rappers] from around the way would battle one another for hours." He noted, "I was good at battling and I practiced it like a sport. I'd spend free time reading the dictionary, building my vocabulary for battles."

One day in 1985, record producer Rodolfo Franklin—better known as DJ Clark Kent—heard teenage Jay-Z battle with other rappers in Marcy. Jay-Z "was incredible," Kent remembered later. "Whenever he rapped with anybody, he outclassed them so bad."

**Ear for talent:** Rodolfo "Clark Kent" Franklin spins records in 2004. DJ Clark Kent was blown away by Jay-Z's early performances.

## Dark Dealings

When Jay-Z was fifteen, a friend approached him with a business opportunity. Many boys they knew were selling crack cocaine—and making a lot of money doing it. The work was illegal and dangerous. Drug dealers carried guns. Shootings between gangs of rival dealers were common. Jay-Z knew the risks, but he also wanted the big money that came along with hustling, as drug dealing was known.

**January 2, 1991**

# 'Gangsta' rap reflects an urban jungle

<u>From the Pages of</u>
<u>USA TODAY</u>

M.C. Hammer and Vanilla Ice may have ended the year topping the pop charts, but "gangsta" rappers— grim storytellers of inner-city violence and sex—rule the rap world. Born in Los Angeles' gang-torn streets, gangsta rap portrays itself as the six o'clock news put to vinyl. The music crackles with gunfire. As gangsta pioneers N.W.A say in "Gangsta, Gangsta": "I got a shotgun, and here's the plot/takin' (expletive) out with a flurry of buckshots."

Last year saw gangsta rap's popularity soar. Ice Cube (*AmeriKKKa's Most Wanted*), Luke featuring the 2 Live Crew (*Banned in the U.S.A.*) and N.W.A (*100 Miles and Runnin'*) made Top 30 on pop charts.

Are they street heroes or negative role models? For a frustrated generation of inner-city youth, they're both. "It's negative in a way, but it lets you know what's going on in reality," says Kevin Lee, 19, of Lake Arbor, MD. "In that sense, it's positive." Says Terrance Thorne, 21, of Capital Heights, MD: "When someone gets on our nerves, I listen to it and think there's enough killing."

Not all gangsta rap is negative. Several acts joined to record "We're All in the Same Gang," an anti-gang song that made *Billboard*'s R & B Top 40 this summer. But the rap offshoot has parents worried. Jamie Brown publishes *Sister to Sister*, a Washington, D.C.-based magazine that covers rap and R & B. She became concerned when one of her two teen sons playfully pointed a finger at her head and recited lyrics from Kool G Rap and D.J. Polo's "Streets of New York:" "I also have a .38."

"I don't even think it's music," Brown says. "It preaches disunity between black males and females, and harming one another physically." Brown has been printing gangsta rap lyrics in her magazine to show parents what their children are hearing. "What bothers me is that it's really their reality," Brown says. "When I saw N.W.A, I thought 'Our children are going through this?' It's good people are made aware of it, but not the kids."

But that's what the kids want to hear, Ice T says. "My stuff is not for the squeamish or very prudish. It is for street people who hang out. They want to hear me," he says, not M.C. Hammer.

—James T. Jones IV

"I wanted money and excitement and loved the idea of cutting myself loose from the rules ... of the straight [law-abiding] world," he later wrote.

Jay-Z began to live a complicated life. He attended Eli Whitney High School and transferred to George Westinghouse High School after Eli Whitney shut down. He was still a rapper. But Jay-Z was also a drug dealer.

He had a friend who dealt crack in Trenton, New Jersey, about an hour away from New York City. On weekends, Jay-Z took the train to Trenton and joined his

**Deadly:** These bags of crack cocaine *(bottom)* and cocaine powder *(top)* were used as evidence in a criminal trial. Jay-Z began dealing crack while in high school.

friend's crew. He found he had a good head for business, a knack for

In addition to Jay-Z, the rappers the Notorious B.I.G. (Christopher Wallace) and Busta Rhymes (Trevor Smith) also attended George Westinghouse High School. They were both a few years younger than Jay-Z.

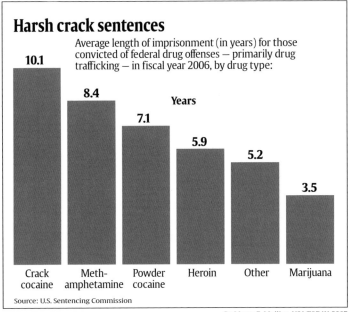

## Harsh crack sentences

Average length of imprisonment (in years) for those convicted of federal drug offenses — primarily drug trafficking — in fiscal year 2006, by drug type:

**Years**

| Crack cocaine | Meth- amphetamine | Powder cocaine | Heroin | Other | Marijuana |
|---|---|---|---|---|---|
| 10.1 | 8.4 | 7.1 | 5.9 | 5.2 | 3.5 |

Source: U.S. Sentencing Commission

By Marcy E. Mullins, USA TODAY, 2007

turning a profit. He never used drugs himself, because he wanted to keep his mind clear and sharp. He and his associates soon expanded their sales territory into Maryland and Virginia. Jay-Z gave up on high school and dropped out.

As a drug dealer, Jay-Z made good money. He helped his mother pay her bills. He also indulged in luxuries for himself, including expensive jewelry and a fancy Lexus. But he was putting his life at risk in the drug business. One time, rival drug dealers shot at him. Another time, he was nearly arrested and put in jail.

Jay-Z was also destroying others' lives by selling them crack. The drug can quickly turn users into addicts. It leaves people with wasted bodies and wasted souls, desperate for their next fix. When Jay-Z was hustling, he didn't consider how much harm he was doing to the people who bought his drugs. He was "so deep in it [the drug-dealing life], and so young, that that type of introspection [self-examination]" didn't happen, he later said.

## One Foot in Each World

Jay-Z's friends in the music world were critical of his choices. They knew he was a tremendous talent. They hated to see him dealing in drugs and death. Jaz-O and others struggled to keep Jay-Z involved in music.

In 1987 Jaz-O and Jay-Z recorded a track on a mixtape—a self-produced album—with rapper Big Daddy Kane (Antonio Hardy). The following year Jaz-O got a record deal with the British music label EMI. EMI sent Jaz-O to London, England, to make his record. Jaz brought Jay-Z with him.

Jay-Z spent most of his time in Brooklyn or Trenton. He had never been on an airplane. He had never visited a foreign country. So the trip to London was a special experience. He and Jaz lived in a London apartment for two months. They rode to a party in a Cadillac limousine. They met British rappers and EMI executives. Jay-Z learned a lot by sitting in on Jaz's recording sessions and meetings. He performed on one track with Jaz, a song called "Hawaiian Sophie."

**Long live the Kane:** Rapper Big Daddy Kane gave Jay-Z an early break by putting him on a 1987 mixtape.

April 21, 2006

# Money in the mixtape

<u>From the Pages of</u>
<u>USA TODAY</u>

Mixtapes long have been part of hip-hop's culture, but the DJ-produced compilations that once existed underground are percolating much closer to the surface these days. The often unlicensed and frequently bootlegged [illegally made] collections of hot street jams, diss songs and freestyles—available for sale via the Internet and street vendors, or as free downloads—aren't just for hardcore fans anymore. They've become promotional tools for artists and record labels trying to build a buzz.

Hip-hop diehards looking to be the first with the latest sounds or seeking edgier material have always scooped up mixtapes. But 50 Cent (Curtis Jackson) is credited with changing the way they are viewed.

In 2001, Columbia Records terminated the budding artist's recording contract. Rather than begging record labels for a new deal, 50 flooded the streets with his own mixtapes and ignited a bidding war between labels trying to sign him. 50's 2003 debut album, *Get Rich or Die Tryin'*, sold 872,000 in its first week.

DJ Clue has been a leading mixtape-maker since 1990—when mixtapes were often still cassette tapes. He has a reputation for exclusives, and gave the streets their first taste of the likes of Jay-Z, DMX, and others. He helped 50 get back on his feet.

"50 Cent and (manager/producer) Sha Money XL were basically outside the radio station every day trying to get their stuff on the radio when they had no buzz," says DJ Clue. "We just kept doing stuff, and he was putting out mixtapes of his own that were hot, and a combination of the two was a lethal combination."

Shanti Das, Universal Motown's executive vice president for marketing and artist development, says the company encourages mixtapes to promote their artists, but that it's important to partner with the right DJs. She says the label often gives DJs exclusive freestyle raps or songs that won't appear on an upcoming mainstream album. The seal of approval from certain DJs gives an artist instant credibility.

"It's about associating with the DJ that has the most influence in a particular market," Das says. "Most mixtapes are released regionally, and it's especially important in hip-hop for an artist to have credibility in their own backyard."

**Game changer:** 50 Cent (Curtis Jackson) scored a record deal and created underground buzz with a series of successful mixtapes.

For many artists, mixtapes are a way to attract the attention of labels increasingly reluctant to invest in finding new artists. Chamillionaire, whose *The Sound of Revenge* was released last year, was known as the Mixtape Messiah in Houston, and sold more than 200,000 copies before Universal signed him. Saigon, who gained notoriety through collaborations with DJ Kay Slay and DJ Whoo Kid, says convincing DJs to put you on their mixtapes and radio shows is the only way to get signed these days. "If you don't have a street buzz where people are talking about you, the record labels aren't interested," Saigon says.

Even established major artists see the value of mixtapes. 50 Cent and his G-Unit troupe keep churning them out on their own, as do other outfits such as D-Block (Jadakiss, Styles P. and Sheek Louch) and Cam'ron's Dipset crew. The platinum duo Mobb Deep (Prodigy and Havoc) has always been rooted in the streets. Despite their mainstream success, they say it's the mixtapes that keep them in touch with their core fans. "You always have to feed your foundation and put that mixtape out there," says Havoc.

Chamillionaire says mixtapes help balance the desire for mainstream success and the need for street credibility. "You can be the biggest star in the world, but there's something about having street respect if you're a rapper," he says. "In some markets, you can have a guy who's all over BET [Black Entertainment Television] and MTV and another guy who is just killing it on mixtapes, and when they get up on stage, you can see the respect the mixtape guy gets."

—Steve Jones

**Jay in the U.K.:** In 1988 Jay-Z visited London, England (seen here in 2011). The trip made a powerful impression on the young rapper.

The stay in London also exposed Jay-Z to some of the more unpleasant aspects of the music industry. Although EMI execs had hosted Jaz-O in the United Kingdom, they weren't happy with his finished record. EMI canceled Jaz's contract. After seeing what happened to his friend, Jay-Z wasn't sure he wanted a career in music. When he got back to the United States, he returned to drug dealing.

But his friends kept pulling him back to hip-hop. Clark Kent took him to parties with open mics—where any rapper could take the microphone and perform. In 1989 Big Daddy Kane invited Jay-Z to go on tour with a group of up-and-coming rap artists, including Queen Latifah (Dana Owens). For four months, the rappers traveled from city to city by bus, putting on shows at clubs. Jay-Z always impressed audiences with his rapid-fire freestyle rhyming. A few years later, Kane asked Jay-Z to rap on his album *Daddy's Home*.

Jay-Z was seeing more and more success as a rapper, but he wasn't ready to give up hustling. He moved back and forth between the two

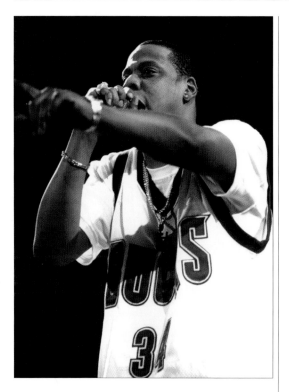

**Two lives:** Jay-Z performs in 1990. At this time, he was uncertain about pursuing a full-time hip-hop career.

worlds—part-time rapping and part-time drug dealing. In 1992 DJ Clark Kent took a position with Atlantic Records. It was his job to scout for new talent. He encouraged Jay-Z to put together a mixtape that he could use to sell himself to Atlantic or another label.

Jay-Z was making big money selling drugs. He wasn't sure he wanted to trade that for a shot at a music career. After all, he had no guarantee of success. But the risks involved with drug dealing were even greater. "I started seeing people go to jail and get killed," he later said, "and the light slowly came on. I was like, 'This life has no good ending.'" Jay-Z was finally ready to give himself 100 percent to music: "I had to leave the streets alone and give it my all."

**Rock-A-Fella founders:** Damon Dash (*left*), Jay-Z, and Kareem Burke (*right*) joined together to form their own record label.

# In Business

■■■■■

Music promoter Damon Dash was on the lookout for new talent. He wanted to find a star, someone with the rhyming skills to land a record deal. If Dash could sign a rap act to a top hip-hop label, such as Def Jam Recordings or Uptown Records—and if the act succeeded—everyone would make money.

Dash knew Clark Kent, who told him that Jay-Z was the rapper he was looking for. Around 1993 Kent set up a meeting and Dash liked what he saw—and liked what he heard of Jay-Z's music. He was eager to promote Jay-Z's career.

Dash scheduled a series of meetings with record executives. Jay-Z, still cautious about the music industry, attended the meetings reluctantly. Although a few executives showed interest, no one came through with a record deal. Both Jay-Z and Dash were frustrated. Jay-Z was tempted to dive back into drug dealing.

To keep Jay-Z focused on music, Dash sent him on tour with a group called Original Flavor. Kareem "Biggs" Burke worked on the tour as a road manager. He and Jay-Z clicked immediately.

Both Dash and Biggs believed in Jay-Z. They knew he could succeed. For his part, Jay-Z still wasn't sure he wanted to work for a record label. He worried that a label would mistreat him the way EMI had mistreated Jaz-O.

Then it dawned on him. Instead of working for a record company, why not start his own label? As Jay-Z later wrote, "When I could really see myself not just rapping but being part of a partnership that would run the whole show, I was ready to take that step."

Dash and Biggs liked the idea of

**Success:** Damon Dash *(left)* and Kareem Burke pose in front of a Bentley, an expensive British car, in 1999.

## What's in a Name?

The name Roc-A-Fella is a play on *Rockefeller*. The Rockefellers are a famous U.S. family. John D. Rockefeller (1839–1937) was a fabulously wealthy businessman. In 1870 he founded Standard Oil, one of the world's first global energy companies. He later created a charity called the Rockefeller Foundation. Many of his descendants also became rich and famous. His grandson Nelson Rockefeller (1908–1979) was governor of New York and vice president of the United States.

By naming their company Roc-A-Fella, Jay-Z, Dash, and Biggs were stating that they would become rich and powerful like the Rockefellers. "We always aspired to have the best, and that name represented the best for us," Jay-Z later said. The name also has a more direct meaning. The label promised to "rock fellows"—that is, to get listeners moving.

**Inspiration:** John D. Rockefeller, pictured here in the 1930s, was extremely rich and successful.

starting a record label. In 1994 the three men agreed to pool their money and go into the music business. Another friend came up with a name: Roc-A-Fella Records.

### Starting from Scratch

The Roc-A-Fella trio drew up a business plan—an outline of how they would launch and run their company. The plan included short- and long-term goals. The first goal was to get a song played on the radio and to get its music video on TV. They wanted to build up buzz about Jay-Z around New York City.

Clark Kent had a studio in his basement, and that's where Roc-A-Fella cut its first track: "I Can't Get with That." They hired Abdul Malik Abbott, a filmmaker, to shoot the music video. It mostly featured Jay-Z rapping in the streets around Marcy Houses, showing off his rhyming skills.

Once the record was pressed and the video was ready, Jay-Z's cousin B-High, Biggs's little brother Hip-Hop, and other friends helped get the music out on the streets. B-High sent the record to DJs at clubs and radio stations. He made sure that Ralph McDaniels got a copy of the video. McDaniels hosted the six-day-a-week *Video Music Box*, a local TV music show.

Jay-Z and the others packed stacks of records into the trunks of their cars. They drove around New York, trying to get music shops to stock the record. They sold the record on consignment. That is, when they dropped off copies at a store, no money changed hands. If a record sold, half the money went to the store and half went back to Roc-A-Fella.

At first, very little money came back into the business, but Roc-A-Fella stuck to its plan. It recorded another song, "In My Lifetime." This song dealt with drug dealing, and the good life that drug money could bring. The video showed Jay-Z

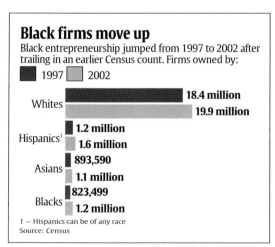

**Black firms move up**

Black entrepreneurship jumped from 1997 to 2002 after trailing in an earlier Census count. Firms owned by:

■ 1997 ▢ 2002

Whites
18.4 million
19.9 million

Hispanics[1]
1.2 million
1.6 million

Asians
893,590
1.1 million

Blacks
823,499
1.2 million

1 — Hispanics can be of any race
Source: Census

By Robert W. Ahrens, USA TODAY, 2005

and his friends partying in the Caribbean, drinking champagne, and driving sports cars. But the video ended on an ominous note. In the last scene, Jay-Z is led from his car by a man in a dark suit, possibly a federal agent.

Instead of selling the "In My Lifetime" single themselves, the Roc-A-Fella team hired a company called Payday to distribute it to stores for them. Jay-Z and the others then rented an office in the financial district of Manhattan, near Wall Street. "In our minds, we were staying close to the money, to Wall Street," Jay-Z later wrote.

Despite its Wall Street location, the Roc-A-Fella office was shabby. It didn't have computers or proper office furniture. The employees mostly hung out on a big leather couch. None of the three partners had any experience running a record label. But they learned on the job. "When we started Roc-A-Fella, we didn't read a book about running a company," Jay-Z once recalled. "We just did what needed to be done."

**Tastemaker:** New York City DJ Funkmaster Flex works a turntable in 2010. Some hip-hop fans heard Jay-Z's "Dead Presidents" for the first time on Flex's radio show.

Damon Dash handled many of the day-to-day duties of managing the company. Jay-Z was also involved in management, but as the label's lead artist, he did the bulk of his work in the recording studio. Kareem Burke was a silent partner, meaning he shared in the profits but had no voice in running the business.

The Roc-A-Fella crew kept pushing Jay-Z's music to DJs. They got a big break in early 1996 when famed New York DJ Funkmaster Flex played one of the songs, "Dead Presidents," on the radio station 97.1 FM—better known as Hot 97. Jay-Z was thrilled when he first heard the song on the radio.

### The First Album

In 1996 Jay-Z moved from Clark Kent's basement studio to D&D Studios in New York. At D&D Jay-Z worked with several producers, including Kent. One day rapper Biggie Smalls (Christopher Wallace, or the Notorious B.I.G.) came through D&D to see Kent. Jay-Z remembered Biggie from George Westinghouse High School. In the studio, the two rappers struck up a fast friendship. Jay-Z invited Biggie to join him on a track he was recording called "Brooklyn's Finest."

**Biggie :** The Notorious B.I.G., seen here in 1995, joined Jay-Z on the 1996 track "Brooklyn's Finest."

While working on "Brooklyn's Finest," Jay-Z and Biggie Smalls became good friends. They planned to collaborate on more music. But in March 1997, Biggie was killed in a drive-by shooting in Los Angeles. He was twenty-four years old. Jay-Z rapped about the senselessness of the killing in his 2003 song "Lucifer."

Jay-Z asked other musician friends to collaborate on other tracks. Mary J. Blige performed on "Can't Knock the Hustle." Memphis Bleek sang on "Coming of Age." Like other rappers, Jay-Z's music sampled existing songs extensively. Sampling involves weaving sections of earlier recordings into the background of a new track or even borrowing the earlier sounds for the new track's hook. On "Politics as Usual," Jay-Z sampled a soul groove from the Stylistics, a 1970s group. "D'Evils" sampled a piano part from the R & B musician Allen Toussaint.

By the middle of 1996, Jay-Z had put together fourteen tracks—enough for a full album. He titled it *Reasonable Doubt*. The album cover featured a photograph of Jay-Z dressed as an old-fashioned gangster, wearing a fedora and a pinkie ring and smoking a cigar.

When the album was ready, Roc-A-Fella hired a company called Priority to handle the distribution. By then, Jay-Z had built name recognition in New York City and beyond. His singles were already being played on the radio and in clubs. So when *Reasonable Doubt* hit stores on June 25, radio stations, music reviewers, and hip-hop fans paid attention.

The reviews were all positive. "What makes these tracks stand out here is the slick way Jay-Z flips lyrics," wrote the *Source*, a hip-hop magazine. "He flows [rhymes] like he's conversing with you at a party or on the street, telling tales of male [sexual] conquest or simple stories of street survival. His lyrics create cuttingly clever rhymes that ride bomb [extraordinary] tracks provided by Clark Kent, Big Jaz [Jaz-O] and others with effortless perfection."

*Rolling Stone*, *Billboard*, and other music publications were equally impressed. Within a year, *Reasonable Doubt* had sold 420,000 copies. With his debut album, Jay-Z had made his name in the world of hip-hop. Roc-A-Fella records had done the same.

**Coming of age:** Jay-Z hangs backstage in 1995. By this time, he had stopped dealing crack and *Reasonable Doubt* was on the way.

**Baller:** Jay-Z poses on the set of a music video in 1999. He enjoyed a series of hits throughout the late 1990s.

# Shot to the Top

■■■■■

With the success of *Reasonable Doubt*, the record companies that had turned Jay-Z down a few years earlier suddenly came knocking. In late 1996, Roc-A-Fella signed a deal with Def Jam, a top hip-hop label. Under the arrangement, Def Jam purchased a 33 percent share of Roc-A-Fella for $1.5 million. Jay-Z, Dash, and Biggs would still run their label as they saw fit, but Def Jam would share the profits with them, with one-third of

**Hip-hop mogul:** Russell Simmons, pictured here in 2007, cofounded the influential record label Def Jam. Rock-A-Fella signed a deal with Def Jam in 1996.

the money going to Def Jam and two-thirds going to Roc-A-Fella. Def Jam would pay to produce Roc-A-Fella's future albums and videos. It also bought the rights to release future copies of *Reasonable Doubt*.

As soon as the deal was done, Jay-Z was back in the studio, at work on a new album. Called *In My Lifetime, Vol. 1*, this 1997 album was slicker and more polished than *Reasonable Doubt*. Many of the songs, such as "The City Is Mine," had a pop music flavor. But other songs, such as "Streets Is Watching" and "Rap Game/Crack Game," were harsh and gritty. On this album, Jay-Z's collaborators included Foxy Brown, Babyface, Lil' Kim, and Sean "Puff Daddy" Combs (later known as Diddy). The samples came from a wide range of musical genres, from the R & B sounds of the O'Jays to the chilly electronic music of German band Kraftwerk to the experimental compositions of Philip Glass.

**Diddy:** Sean Combs *(pictured)* collaborated with Jay-Z on the album *In My Lifetime, Vol. 1.*

The reviewers didn't rave about *In My Lifetime* the way they had about *Reasonable Doubt*, but the record still sold more than one million copies. It reached No. 3 on the *Billboard 200*, a weekly ranking of top-selling albums by *Billboard* magazine. Jay-Z had become a full-fledged hip-hop star.

## Hard Knocks

Riding a wave of success, Jay-Z quickly put out another album, *Vol. 2 . . . Hard Knock Life*, in 1998. The title song, "Hard

# IN F⬤CUS

## The Beat and the Flow

Hip-hop music consists of two main parts: the beat and the flow. The beat is the background rhythm, created by instruments or just by the clapping of hands. In the studio, producers create beats using synthesizers, drum machines, samples, and loops (short segments of music played on repeat).

The flow is what comes from the rapper's mouth—the rhymes. At any given time during the course of a song, the flow might sync up with the background rhythm or it might follow a beat of its own. Jay-Z once explained it this way: "The flow isn't like time, it's like life. It's like a heartbeat or the way you breathe, it can jump, speed up, slow down, stop, or pound right through like a machine."

Knock Life (Ghetto Anthem)," was unusual for hip-hop music. It didn't sample from rap, rock, or R & B. It sampled from the Broadway musical *Annie*.

Jay-Z had seen the film version of *Annie* on TV when he was a little boy. The movie, based on the *Little Orphan Annie* comic strip, tells the story of a young girl named Annie who hopes to leave her city orphanage. Young Jay-Z identified with the film's orphan girls, who were poor and often mistreated. "These kids sing about the hard knock life, things everyone in the ghetto feels coming [growing] up," Jay-Z explained later.

"Hard Knock Life (Ghetto Anthem)" features Jay-Z rapping about guns, hustling, and ghetto life between a chorus of little girls singing the original "Hard Knock Life," sampled from the Broadway show recording. This unexpected coupling of musical styles added up to a big hit. Some people who had never listened to hip-hop before became fans after hearing "Hard Knock Life." When Jay-Z performed the song

**Rags to riches:** The musical *Annie* tells the story of an orphan who escapes poverty. It inspired one of Jay-Z's most popular songs, "Hard Knock Life (Ghetto Anthem)."

**On top:** Jay-Z rocks the mic in Washington, D.C., during his 1999 Hard Knock Life Tour.

at live shows, audience members would join in joyously on the chorus.

Based on the popularity of "Hard Knock Life (Ghetto Anthem)" and other songs, *Vol. 2...Hard Knock Life* eventually sold five million copies in the United States. The album launched Jay-Z even higher into the hip-hop stratosphere. The record also made Jay-Z and his business partners rich. At the Grammy Awards—a yearly ceremony honoring top musical artists—*Vol. 2...Hard Knock Life* was named the best rap album of 1998.

When Jay-Z was recording tracks in the 1990s, his musician friends were amazed to see that he kept all his lyrics in his head. They joked that he must be a religious visionary. They called him Jay-Hova, which came from Jehovah (God). Jay-Z shortened that nickname to Hova.

## Empire Builders

Jay-Z, Damon Dash, and Biggs Burke had big dreams. They loved producing music, but they were interested in other business ventures as well. Dash wanted to make films. Under his direction, Roc-A-Fella spun off a new business, Roc-A-Fella Films. In 1998 the company released a DVD called *Streets Is Watching*. The film featured a series of Jay-Z's music videos woven around a few nonmusical scenes. In 1999 the company made a movie called *Backstage*. This film followed Jay-Z on his Hard Knock Life Tour, which took him (with fellow artists Beanie Sigel, DMX, and others) to nearly fifty cities for live shows.

In 1999 Roc-A-Fella also launched a clothing line called Rocawear. The company teamed up with existing clothing manufacturers to produce men's T-shirts, jeans, jackets, and other items. It soon expanded into women's clothing, kids' clothing, footwear, accessories, and even a men's cologne, 9IX. With Rocawear, the Roc-A-Fella team had another hit on their hands. After eighteen months in business, Rocawear took in $80 million in revenue.

**New talent:** Damon Dash *(center right)* stands with members of the 2004 Rock-A-Fella roster, all wearing Rocawear. The label grew quickly after Jay-Z's first hits.

**June 25, 1999**

# Hip-hop takes the high road

<u>From the Pages of
USA TODAY</u>

When the Sugar Hill Gang hit the airwaves 20 years ago with "Rapper's Delight," rap music was quickly dismissed as a fad that would be gone within six months. But despite critics—political and artistic—and periodic crises, the art form has kept growing. According to the Recording Industry Association of America, rap and R & B outsell every genre of music except rock, which has sharply declined over the past decade.

**Educator:** In 1999 Grammy-winner Lauryn Hill brought new listeners to hip-hop.

The influence doesn't end with the succession of chart-topping and multi-platinum hip-hop albums. The music and its stars are used to sell everything from jeans to soda pop to sports teams, and they've injected terms like jiggy and scrubs into the popular lexicon.

In February, Lauryn Hill collected five Grammy Awards, a record for a female artist. When *Forbes* published its list of highest-paid entertainers in December, rapper/moguls Master P and Sean "Puffy" Combs were near the top of the list for musicians. And for the third time in four years, a Will Smith blockbuster will begin packing movie theaters on the Fourth of July weekend.

Lyor Cohen, who with label founder Russell Simmons helped build Def Jam Recordings into hip-hop's most enduring label, says the music is to '90s youth what rock 'n' roll was in the '50s and '60s.

"It is an incredibly flourishing art form that is captivating teen-agers and annoying parents," says Cohen. "You would be surprised how mainstream hip-hop has been for years, selling millions and millions of records. But because it was always lumped into urban market share (with R&B), it was completely beneath the (media's) radar."

Damon Dash, CEO of Rock-A-Fella Records, says that hip-hop is "the pulse of the street. For a long time people didn't understand that. They thought it was just glorifying violence or a fun way of life because they didn't want to take the time to listen. But as long as there's struggle, there'll be hip-hop."

Hip-hop itself has had to struggle at times. For years, naysayers waited for it to disappear, while critics wished it would. A frequent target of politicians, it has had to fend off all manner of attempts to curtail or legislate it. And it has had its share of internecine battles and wasteful tragedies (the slayings of Tupac Shakur and the Notorious B.I.G. among them). But despite all that, this urban-born music has survived and flourished, broadening its audience from mostly black fans to a multiethnic following that is 70% white and cuts across all economic, social and geographical lines.

"It's incredible the way it's influencing America, not just black America," rap veteran Heavy D says. "You have suburban kids using everything from the fashion to the slang, and it's bringing people together without racial barriers."

"I remember when people were saying that rap wasn't going to last, but it has a language that they can talk, and it's so real," says Erick Sermon, producer and half of the seminal rap duo EPMD. "What kid wouldn't want to be down with something so hip?"

Chuck D, leader of the groundbreaking band Public Enemy, says hip-hop's infusion into the mainstream is the natural result of its prolonged exposure via videos. "Ten years ago, *Yo MTV Raps!* kicked rap all across America. Kids as young as 6 or 7 then grew up with the music. So what you have is a culture that is synonymous with people from more than just the race that it came from."

"Once hip-hop culture enters your life, it's hard to get away from it," says Jermaine Dupri, producer and CEO of Atlanta-based So So Def Records. "It's the dress, the language and everything that goes with it. It has really hit home now, and that's why (Detroit rapper) Eminem can come out now and nobody is talking about (the validity of) white rappers."

—Steve Jones

# IN FOCUS

## Trouble with the Law

*Vol. 3...The Life and Times of S. Carter* was scheduled for release in December 1999. But more than a month ahead of the release date, bootlegged copies of the album somehow got into stores. This was serious business. Bootlegging can cost a record label millions of dollars in lost sales.

Jay-Z asked around and was told that record producer Lance "Un" Rivera had been making the bootleg copies. Furious, Jay-Z confronted Rivera at a party at the Kit Kat Club in Manhattan. A fight broke out, and Jay-Z plunged a knife into Rivera's stomach. (Rivera was not seriously wounded.) The next day, Jay-Z turned himself in to police.

The case took several years to work its way through the legal system. The original charge was felony assault, a serious crime. With the help of his lawyer, Jay-Z had the charge reduced to the less serious misdemeanor assault. His punishment was three years' probation. Rivera's involvement with the bootlegging has not been proven.

**Feud:** Jay-Z assaulted record producer Lance Rivera *(left)* in 1999, after hearing rumors that Rivera had made illegal copies of the album *Vol. 3 . . . The Life and Times of S. Carter.* Right: Jay-Z leaves the courthouse in 2001.

### The Dynasty

Jay-Z released his fourth album, *Vol. 3...The Life and Times of S. Carter*, in 1999. This album contained the bouncy hit "Big Pimpin'," a collaboration with the southern hip-hop crew UGK. In the first week after its release, *Life and Times* sold five hundred thousand copies. Within the year, the sales total was three million. *Rolling Stone* magazine proclaimed, "This is [Jay-Z's] strongest album to date, with music that's filled with catchy hooks, rump-shaking beats and lyrics fueled by Jay's hustler's vigilance."

In 2000 Jay-Z released *The Dynasty: Roc La Familia*. On the album cover, Jay-Z posed with his hands in front of his face. His thumbs and forefingers were held together to form a diamond—his symbol for the Roc-A-Fella music dynasty.

*Dynasty* featured a lot of rapping by Beanie Sigel and Memphis Bleek. It also contained the soulful "This Can't Be Life," with beats by Kanye West, then an unknown producer from Chicago.

**Diamond:** Jay-Z holds up the Roc-A-Fella diamond symbol at the 2000 Radio Music Awards.

December 27, 1999

# Rapper Jay-Z is pulling no punches

From the Pages of
<u>USA TODAY</u> Jay-Z sits at the studio console, bobbing his head to the beat thumping from the speakers on the wall in front of him. He concentrates on the track, quietly mouthing words to himself. Satisfied, he turns to engineer Chauncey Mahan and says, "OK, I'm ready."

As he leaves the room and heads for the recording booth, rapper Beanie Sigel, who has watched the whole thing from the black leather couch behind them, shakes his head in wonder. "You've just witnessed something amazing and probably don't even realize it," Sigel says. "He's just come up with a song, the hook, everything, while he was sitting there."

The rhymes Jay-Z has composed in his head begin flowing out of the speakers as if he has rehearsed for days. But it's all happening spontaneously. Unlike the many rappers who live by their pens and pads, Jay-Z never puts anything down on paper.

"I don't write songs," says Jay-Z, 29, whose 1998 album *Vol. 2 . . . Hard Knock Life* has sold close to 5 million copies. "I just sit there and listen to the track, and I come up with the words. It's a gift. A gift from God."

That gift, which includes melding hard-core street sensibilities with mass pop appeal, will be put to the test Tuesday with the release of *The Life & Times of Shawn Carter . . . Vol. 3*, his fourth album since 1996 and the one he says will show whether people really like Jay-Z or have just been caught up in the hype surrounding his phenomenal rise. Expectations are extremely high: The album not only is poised for one

The big hit off the album was the playful "I Just Wanna Love U (Give It 2 Me)," on which singer-producer Pharrell Williams joined Jay-Z. As usual with Jay-Z's albums, *Dynasty* flew off store shelves. The release debuted at No. 1 on the *Billboard* charts and sold more than 550,000 copies in a week.

of the year's biggest opening weeks, but has a shot at becoming the first No. 1 of the new millennium.

Jay-Z's fans are well aware of his pre-rap life as a cocaine dealer, which he has talked about in interviews. Many of his songs deal with the risks and consequences of criminal activities. That "realness" has always been part of his appeal.

"It makes up my music, and that's why you've got titles like 'Hard Knock Life,'" says Jay-Z, who grew up the youngest of four children in Brooklyn's Marcy Projects, where the J and Z subway trains run. "It's about my struggles and the things I've seen and the things I've been around."

Aside from his own album, Jay-Z will be busy next year getting albums by Roc-a-Fella artists Sigel, Memphis Bleek and Amil on the market. The company also launched a clothing line this year and has two Miramax-distributed films in the works. One is a documentary about his tour, *Backstage*. The second is an untitled film about three Harlem hustlers.

Part of the reason that he's able to keep people from tiring of him—and probably the key to his crossover appeal—is that he never seems to repeat himself. He goes for unusual beats (the futuristic "Can I Get A . . . ," the salsa-laced "Girls' Best Friend") and adjusts his rap flows to match them. For "Hard Knock Life," he used the bratty chorus of the theme from the Broadway musical *Annie* (a favorite since childhood because his sister is named Annie) to tell his own underdog tale.

"I like to bring different things into the game rather than just go for the same old hot beat," he says. "I'm thinking . . . how can I take it one step further, and how can I get people to sing along and make sure that they enjoy the music they buy?"

Now the question is whether the public is still eager to buy what he has to offer. In 1998, he put out a direct-to-video film and soundtrack titled *Streets Is Watching*. They were then, and they are now. And so is just about everybody else. Because of success "people think that things change with you and start treating you differently. . . . But I'm the same dude . . . still holding firm in my position."

—Steve Jones

Jay-Z's energy and output was enormous. *The Dynasty: Roc La Familia* was his fifth album in five years. "I could make records as long as I have the desire to really dig deep and challenge myself to do it," he told a reporter for *Vibe* magazine. "I can do it for as long as I want."

# CHAPTER FIVE

**Buddies:** Jay-Z and Kanye West *(right)* hit the red carpet for the premiere of Jay-Z's 2004 concert film. West has produced Jay-Z songs on albums such as *The Blueprint.*

# Millions

By 2001 Roc-A-Fella had established itself as a major hip-hop label. Roc-A-Fella had signed other rappers, including Beanie Sigel and Memphis Bleek, but Jay-Z was the star of the show. He continued to pump out records at the rate of one per year.

In 2001 Kanye West moved to New York to work with Roc-A-Fella full-time. He did most of the production work on Jay-Z's next album, *The Blueprint.* With this album, Jay-Z once again scored big. Hit songs included

"Takeover," which sampled the 1960s rock band the Doors, and "Izzo (H.O.V.A.)," which sampled "I Want You Back" by the Jackson 5. Only one song on the album had a guest artist, the rapper Eminem, who joined Jay-Z on "Renegade."

Once again, sales were enormous and critics raved. The songs on *The Blueprint* are "stunning, to the point where the album seems almost flawless," wrote one reviewer. "Besides rhymes that challenge those on *Reasonable Doubt* . . . in terms of not only lyrics but also flow and delivery, *The Blueprint* also boasts some of his most extravagant beats." *The Blueprint* was "a fully realized masterpiece," the reviewer concluded.

The song "Takeover" stirred up trouble within the New York hip-hop scene. Earlier in 2001, the rapper Nas (Nasir Jones) had insulted Jay-Z in one of his songs, calling him a fake. On "Takeover," Jay-Z struck back, hurling his own insults at Nas. Nas retaliated with more

**The illest:** Nas performs at a 2012 summer concert festival. Nas and Jay-Z were rivals for several years.

# IN F CUS

## Going Platinum

Many of Jay-Z's albums have "gone platinum." Other records are said to "go gold" or "go diamond." These terms refer to sales numbers. An album that sells five hundred thousand copies is called a gold record. An album that sells a million copies is a platinum record. The rare album that sells ten million copies is a diamond record. The Recording Industry Association of America tracks album sales and hands out honors to artists for gold, platinum, and diamond records.

put-downs of Jay-Z on his song "Ether," and Jay-Z fought back on "Supa Ugly," a freestyle track. The musical sparring created publicity—and higher record sales—for both artists.

### The Good Life

Jay-Z had gone from rags to riches. He was worth millions of dollars. He owned fancy cars and lived in a luxury apartment in Manhattan. He was grateful for his wealth and wanted to share some of it with people who were less fortunate. In 2002 he established the Shawn Carter Scholarship Foundation, to help pay for low-income students to attend college. Jay-Z's mother, Gloria, took charge of the foundation.

At Roc-A-Fella, the money kept rolling in. Although Roc-A-Fella Films didn't see success, business boomed at Rocawear. And of course, money poured in from record sales. Jay-Z showed no signs of slowing down. He got to work on his next album, 2002's *The Blueprint 2: The Gift and the Curse*. The release was a two-CD set, with twenty-five songs in all.

For one song on the album, "'03 Bonnie & Clyde," Jay-Z collaborated with Beyoncé Knowles, lead singer of the vocal group Destiny's

Child. "'03 Bonnie and Clyde" is a love song, with Beyoncé wrapping smooth R & B vocals around Jay-Z's rougher rap lyrics. The original Bonnie and Clyde—Bonnie Parker and Clyde Barrow—were 1930s bank robbers and lovers who fled from the law. In the video, Jay-Z and Beyoncé are also sweethearts and fugitives from the law. They flee to Mexico by car.

Jay-Z worked with Beyoncé again later that year. On her first solo album, *Dangerously in Love*, he rapped on the song "Crazy in Love." Early in 2003, at the Grammys, that song won two awards: Best R & B Song and Best Rap/ Sung Collaboration. Around this time, Jay-Z and Beyoncé took their collaboration beyond the recording studio and started dating, but they tried to keep their romance private.

**Father and Son**

For more than twenty years, Jay-Z had had no contact with his father, A. J., who had left the family around 1981. But Jay-Z's mother, Gloria,

**Power couple:** Jay-Z duets with Beyoncé at the 2003 MTV Video Music Awards. For a time, the couple kept their relationship a secret.

# IN F⊙CUS

## Jay-Z's Grammys

Alone and with collaborators, Jay-Z has won American Music Awards, MTV Video Music Awards, People's Choice Awards, BET Awards, and many others. He has also won nine Grammy Awards and counting:

| Year | Song/Album | Grammy Award |
|------|------------|--------------|
| 1998 | *Vol. 2 . . . Hard Knock Life* | Best Rap Album |
| 2003 | "Crazy in Love" | Best Rap/Sung Collaboration (with Beyoncé Knowles) |
| 2003 | "Crazy in Love" | Best R&B Song |
| 2004 | "99 Problems" | Best Rap Solo Performance |
| 2008 | "Swagga Like Us" | Best Rap Performance by a Duo or Group |
| 2009 | "Run This Town" | Best Rap/Sung Collaboration (with Kanye West and Rihanna) |
| 2009 | "D.O.A. (Death of Auto-Tune)" | Best Rap Solo Performance |
| 2010 | "Empire State of Mind" | Best Rap/Sung Collaboration (with Alicia Keys) |
| 2010 | "On to the Next One" | Best Rap Performance by a Duo or Group (with Swizz Beatz) |

stayed in touch with her ex-husband. In 2003 she told Jay-Z that his dad had liver disease and was likely to die soon. She wanted father and son to spend some time together. Jay-Z was reluctant. He still resented his father for leaving when he was a boy, but he agreed to a meeting.

The first time Gloria arranged a meeting, A. J. didn't show up. Jay-Z was angry, but he still agreed to a second meeting. This one went off as planned. "Me and my pop got to talk," Jay-Z remembered later. "I got to let it [the anger] go. I got to tell him everything I wanted to say. I just said what I felt. It wasn't yelling and crying and drastic and dramatic. It was very adult and grown men, but it was tough. I didn't let him off the hook." At the end of the meeting, A. J. apologized and Jay-Z forgave his father.

Once Jay-Z had cleared the air with his dad, he felt a great sense of peace. He rented his father an apartment in Brooklyn and bought furniture to make it homey. Jay-Z hoped to help A. J. recover his health, but the illness was too far along. A. J. died a few months after reconciling with his son. After A. J. died, Jay-Z wrote a song called "Moment of Clarity." In it he rapped about making peace with his father.

### Show Business

Musically, 2003 was a busy year for Jay-Z. He recorded tracks for his eighth album, *The Black Album*. On one track, Jay-Z got his mother, Gloria, into the act. Jay-Z brought her into the studio one day, turned on the tape recorder, and asked her to tell stories about his life. Gloria

**Still close:** Jay-Z and his mother, Gloria Carter, appear at an event for the Shawn Carter Foundation in 2011.

spoke about Jay-Z's birth, noting that he weighed a hefty 10.5 pounds (4.8 kilograms) upon arrival. She also told of how he learned to ride a bike at the age of four, how he withdrew emotionally after his father left, and how he rapped at all hours of the day and night as a teenager.

Jay-Z added his own raps to the track, which he called "December 4th"—his birthday. The background beats, created by producer Just Blaze, sampled the 1970s R & B group the Chi-Lites. This choice was another callback to the sound track of Jay-Z's Brooklyn childhood. Another song on *The Black Album,* "99 Problems," was notable for its heavy guitar hook as well as its backstory. On one verse, Jay-Z tells the tale of getting pulled over by a police officer—supposedly for speeding but mainly for being young and black. The officer wants to search the car for guns and drugs, but the driver knows his rights and refuses to allow the search. Jay-Z's song about his father, "Moment of Clarity," also made the album.

Meanwhile, Jay-Z had a number of business deals in the works. Companies knew well that when Jay-Z drank a certain brand of champagne in a video or wore a certain brand of clothing onstage, sales of that product took a dramatic jump. The producer of athletic shoes and sportswear Reebok wanted to get in on that action. It worked with Jay-Z to create a line of men's sneakers called the S. Carter Collection. The

**Shoes to fill:** Jay-Z takes a question at a press conference announcing the release of the S. Carter footwear collection in 2003.

leather sneakers came in several different designs and a variety of color combinations. The name "S. Carter" was displayed prominently on the shoes, and Jay-Z appeared in ads to promote them. At $150 a pair, the sneakers were pricey. But as a bonus for buyers, each pair came with a CD containing samples from Jay-Z's upcoming *The Black Album*. When the sneakers arrived at stores in April 2003, sales were tremendous. Across the United States, ten thousand pairs sold in the first hour alone.

In another business venture, Jay-Z and two partners, Desiree Gonzalez and Juan Perez, launched the 40/40 Club, a sports bar in the Flatiron District of Manhattan. The club opened in June 2003. Soon after Jay-Z and rapper 50 Cent embarked on a Rock the Mic Tour. The tour took them to cities all over the United States.

## Black Out

At a press conference on September 25, 2003, Jay-Z told reporters that he was retiring. He said that *The Black Album* would be his last full-length album and that he'd be kicking off a farewell tour on November 25 at Madison Square Garden in New York.

**Making headlines:** Jay-Z and Russell Simmons *(right)* reveal plans for Jay-Z's "retirement," which began with a concert at New York City's Madison Square Garden in November 2003.

**June 27, 2003**

# Jay-Z's 40/40 sports bar
# covers all the bases

<u>From the Pages of</u>
<u>USA TODAY</u>

When it comes to sports, rap mogul Jay-Z knows the score. He loves basketball. Digs football. And brags that his S. Carter sneaker (Jay-Z's real name: Shawn Carter) was the fastest-selling debut in Reebok history. "I'm not an athlete, and that's an amazing feat!" grins Jay-Z. "Get it?"

Yeah, we sure do. And now Jay-Z can savor sports in high style at his 40/40 bar, a spaciously luxe lounge at 6 W. 25th St., right near Madison Square Park. The bar gets its name from the elite baseball players—Barry Bonds, Jose Canseco and Alex Rodriguez—who have hit 40 home runs and stolen 40 bases in a single season.

Last week's opening party drew an athletic A-list, including Magic Johnson, the New Jersey Nets' Jason Kidd, high school sensation LeBron James, as well as actress Chloe Sevigny and, of course, Jay-Z's 21-year-old girlfriend, Beyoncé Knowles.

"Most sports clubs are really dumps," says Jay-Z, 33. "And I never had a spot where guys and girls can get together and go somewhere. I've been there every day. It's like a clubhouse for me. I can go there and relax."

But don't expect to run into Jay-Z while you're chowing down on wings or miniburgers in the playas' paradise, which includes a cigar room, televisions and lounges with pool tables. The boss doesn't tend bar or work the floor; instead, he hangs at one of the two upstairs VIP rooms, where he watches sports or eats the upscale bar food cooked up by his own former personal chef, Cynthia Sestito.

Jay-Z, who in addition to his bling-blinging music biz runs Roc-A-Wear clothing and Roc-A-Fella Films, is back in the studio working on the follow-up to *The Blueprint*. He's recording in spurts, he says, a process made easier by the fact that his studio is in the same neighborhood as 40/40.

And although he says he won't comment at all on his love life, he might do another duet with "'03 Bonnie and Clyde" collaborator Knowles, who just released her own solo debut, *Dangerously in Love*. "Depends on how hot her album is," he laughs.

—Donna Freydkin

Reporters and Jay-Z fans didn't take the announcement too seriously. Many other artists had announced their retirements, only to be lured back to the mic by the love of music.

Meanwhile, fans eagerly awaited the release of *The Black Album*. When it hit stores in mid-November, it immediately flew to the top of the *Billboard* 200. The album was nominated for a Grammy for Best Rap Album, and "99 Problems" was nominated for Best Solo Rap Performance.

Later in November, the Madison Square Garden show was a sellout. As a boy, Jay-Z had gone to the Garden to watch New York

**Champion:** Jay-Z shows up in style to his sold-out Madison Square Garden concert on November 25, 2003.

Knicks basketball games with his dad. As a teenage rapper, he had dreamed of performing there one day. That day had finally arrived. Seeing his name on the marquee before the show was a special thrill for Jay-Z.

To open the show, bells clanged and a boxing announcer boomed out, "Ladies and gentlemen. Tonight we've come to Madison Square Garden, New York City, to see and hear a legendary superstar.... Presenting the one, the only, undisputed, undefeated heavyweight champion of the world of hip-hop, he is . . . JAY-Z."

Jay-Z appeared onstage in a swirl of white smoke. That evening he performed many of his greatest hits. A host of guest performers— Missy Elliot, Twista, Beyoncé, Foxy Brown, Mary J. Blige, R. Kelly, and others—joined him on various songs. The audience couldn't have been more delighted.

Jay-Z was at the top of his game. It wasn't clear where he was headed next, but it was clear that—retirement or no—no one had heard the last from him.

## Executive Suite

In 2004 Jay-Z was just as busy as ever. Although he had stopped work on solo albums, he recorded *Collision Course*, a collaborative album with the rap-rock group Linkin Park. He also recorded *Unfinished Business*, a collaborative album with R & B singer R. Kelly. Before the album came out, he and Kelly hit the road for the Unfinished Business Tour. The duo performed in twenty-three cities.

Jay-Z was always on the lookout for new business opportunities. So when he got the chance to buy a stake in a professional basketball team, he jumped on it. A group of investors wanted to buy the New Jersey Nets and move the team to Brooklyn, Jay-Z's hometown. Jay-Z loved the National Basketball Association (NBA) and loved the idea of owning a team—especially one that was slated to play in Brooklyn. Jay-Z put money in with the investment group, and in 2004, the deal

The 2004 film *Fade to Black* captures the magic and energy of a live Jay-Z show. *Fade to Black* is a documentary about Jay-Z's "retirement" concert at Madison Square Garden in November 2003. Fans who weren't lucky enough to attend the show in person can enjoy it by watching the movie.

**Collision:** Jay-Z shares the stage with Chester Bennington *(right),* singer for the rap-rock group Linkin Park, at the 2006 Grammy Awards.

went through. The move to Brooklyn would not happen for several years, however.

Big changes were happening at Roc-A-Fella as well. Def Jam already owned 33 percent of the company. In 2004 Def Jam paid $10 million to purchase the remaining portion of Roc-A-Fella. Then executives at the Universal Music Group, Def Jam's parent company, made Jay-Z an exciting offer. Universal execs recognized that Jay-Z was a clever businessman. They knew he was at the cutting edge of hip-hop culture. Hoping he could breathe new excitement into the label, Universal asked Jay-Z to become president of Def Jam, with a salary of $8 to $10 million a year.

As president, Jay-Z would be able to sign new artists and determine Def Jam's musical direction. Jimmy Iovine, head of the Universal's Interscope label, explained why Jay-Z was the right person for the job: "He's a talent, he's a talent finder, he's a record maker, he's a magnet, he's creative, he's smart. He's the modern record guy. He's got great feel, he's got great taste, and he knows how to market."

# IN FOCUS

## The Brooklyn Nets: For Better or Worse

Moving the New Jersey Nets to Brooklyn was a controversial project. The person behind the move was businessman Bruce Ratner. Ratner bought the Nets in 2004 and then sold ownership shares to Jay-Z and others. Many people, including Jay-Z, were happy to hear that Brooklyn was going to have a professional sports team—the first pro team in the borough since the Dodgers baseball team left in 1957. Others were upset by the news.

Along with moving the team to Brooklyn, Ratner planned to build a 22-acre (9-hectare) development called the Atlantic Yards. The yards would include a sports arena called the Barclays Center, plus stores, offices, and apartment buildings. To make room for the complex, many old Brooklyn houses and commercial buildings had to be knocked down. People who lived and worked in the area fought in court to stop the project. They wanted to save their neighborhood from the wrecking ball, but the courts ruled against them. The project went through.

The Barclays Center was completed in 2012. Other buildings will be completed over a twenty-five-year period. The Brooklyn Nets played their first game in the Barclays Center in the fall of 2012.

**No. 9 :** Marshon Brooks (*right*) of the Brooklyn Nets take a shot over an opponent during an NBA summer league basketball game in 2012.

Jay-Z believed that he would be a good fit for the job too. He accepted the offer.

For several years, Jay-Z had been clashing with Damon Dash about management issues at Roc-A-Fella. And with Jay-Z taking on the president's job at Def Jam, he would automatically become Dash's boss. This arrangement didn't sit well with Dash. He decided to break his ties with Roc-A-Fella and start a new record label. Jay-Z also purchased Dash's stake in the

**Strained friendship:** Damon Dash *(left)* and Jay-Z pose together at the launch of Jay-Z's 40/40 Club in 2003, one year before Dash left Roc-A-Fella.

Rocawear business for $22 million. After ten years in business together, Jay-Z and Dash officially ended their partnership. Kareem Burke left Roc-A-Fella at this time as well.

USA TODAY
A GANNETT COMPANY

# CHAPTER SIX

**Hip-hop royalty:** Jay-Z meets Charles, Prince of Wales (*left*), during a 2004 trip to London, England.

# Mr. President

In January 2005, Jay-Z settled into a posh twenty-ninth-floor office at Def Jam headquarters in midtown Manhattan. The window gave him a spectacular view across the Hudson River. The office was outfitted with expensive furniture and a high-end sound system. On one wall, Jay-Z hung a picture of himself hobnobbing with Prince Charles, heir to the British throne, at an event in London. But on the floor in one corner of the office, Jay-Z placed a reminder of his more humble beginnings. It was a street sign that read "Marcy Ave." That sign reminded Jay-Z how far he had come.

Def Jam Records was royalty in the world of hip-hop music. Founded in 1984 by Russell Simmons and Rick Rubin, the label had produced such rap legends as LL Cool J, the Beastie Boys, and Public Enemy. But by the time Jay-Z took over as president, the label was stale. It needed new energy. As Jay-Z remembered later, "There was nothing fresh, no excitement.... I said, 'Where's the passion? Where's the ideas?'"

Jay-Z wanted to get the staff fired up. He arranged for a two-day retreat at a fancy New York hotel. He went around the room, asking each person to recall why he or she had chosen to work in the music business. He played a tape of a Def Jam sales presentation from 1984. The presentation captured the spirit of the company when it was young and hungry. It made the employees say, "Wow, I feel proud to work at Def Jam," recalled one senior vice president.

Jay-Z got to work signing new artists. He signed rapper Young Jeezy, R & B singer Ne-Yo, and the hip-hop/soul band the Roots. He also signed Rihanna, a young singer from Barbados who wowed

**Sharing the spotlight:** Jay-Z backs up Rihanna *(right)* onstage in 2012. Rihanna is one of several talented performers Jay-Z signed while serving as president of Def Jam.

fans with her 2005 smash hit "Pon De Replay." Meanwhile, Jay-Z oversaw the work of existing Def Jam/Roc-A-Fella artists, including Ludacris, Kanye West, and Young Gunz.

At home Jay-Z lived the life of a true music mogul. By then he owned two multimillion-dollar apartments in Manhattan, plus one in New Jersey. He owned one of the world's most luxurious and expensive cars, a Mercedes Maybach, and employed a driver to sit behind the wheel. He had a time-share account with a jet company. When he wanted to travel out of town, he, Beyoncé, and his friends and business associates could travel in privacy in a spacious thirteen-seat jet.

## Bad News

Although life was grand for Jay-Z, he also had to face tragedy. In the summer of 2005, his nephew Colleek Luckie (his sister Annie's son) was killed in a car crash in Pennsylvania. Jay-Z was devastated.

Later in the summer, Hurricane Katrina struck the Gulf Coast of

# IN FOCUS

## The Power of Words

Some people are offended by the rough language of hip-hop. Rappers often use curse words, as well as racial or sexual epithets (slurs). Hip-hop CDs often carry "parental advisory" labels to warn parents that the language on an album or a single might not be appropriate for their children.

Jay-Z's success and popularity have made him into a spokesperson for hip-hop. At times he has had to address the concerns over the music's strong language. In the case of racially charged language, he argues that words are only hateful when they are said with hate. He explains that by embracing certain racial epithets, rappers have helped remove the terms' hateful meanings.

**After Katrina:** Many homes and businesses in New Orleans were damaged or destroyed when Hurricane Katrina hit the city in 2005.

the United States. The hurricane flooded the city of New Orleans, Louisiana. As floodwaters rose in the city, thousands of people—mostly poor African Americans who had no way to leave the city ahead of time—climbed into attics and onto rooftops. The U.S. government was slow to help the people stranded in New Orleans. Several thousand drowned. Thousands more lost their homes.

Jay-Z donated $1 million to help assist the victims of Hurricane Katrina. Meanwhile, his friend and producer Kanye West publicly criticized U.S. president George W. Bush for reacting slowly and neglecting the black victims of Hurricane Katrina.

Kanye took a lot of flak for knocking Bush, but Jay-Z supported his friend 100 percent. He reflected later, "He [Kanye] was expressing a feeling that was bottled up in a lot of our hearts. It didn't feel like Katrina was just a natural disaster that randomly swept through a corner of the United States. Katrina felt like something that was happening to black people, specifically. I know all sorts of people [different ethnic groups] in Louisiana and Mississippi got washed out, too, and saw their lives destroyed—but . . . I felt hurt in a personal way for those [African American] people floating on cars and waving on the roofs of their . . . houses, crying into the cameras for help, being left on their porches. Maybe I felt some sense of shame that we'd let this happen to our brothers and sisters."

Jay-Z later wrote about Hurricane Katrina in 2006 a song called "Minority Report." He too criticized President Bush and the government on the track, but he also berated himself for giving only money to help the hurricane victims. He said that a more meaningful contribution would have been a gift of his time—meeting with victims and helping them in person.

 Jay-Z loves pro basketball. He's part owner of the Brooklyn Nets and is friends with NBA players such as LeBron James of the Miami Heat. Jay-Z's favorite player is Michael Jordan, who led the Chicago Bulls to six championships in the 1990s. He even calls himself the Michael Jordan of Recordin'.

## Peace Pact

Jay-Z's duties at Def Jam kept him behind a desk for much of the day, but he also made time for his own music. On October 27, 2005, Jay-Z gave a concert at the Continental Airlines Arena in New Jersey, where the New Jersey Nets played basketball. Jay-Z called the show the I Declare War concert and announced ahead of time that he would attack some rival rappers at the event.

**Declaring peace:** In October 2005, Jay-Z and Nas *(left)* ended their feud while onstage in East Rutherford, New Jersey.

At the arena, the stage was set up like the Oval Office—the president's office in the White House. A rug on the floor was decorated with the presidential seal. Two men dressed as Secret Service agents stood at the back of the stage. The concert featured many guest artists, including Ne-Yo, Young Jeezy, and Kanye West. A DJ spun records to provide the beats.

As the evening wore on, the audience enjoyed the show, but there were no signs of war with other rappers. Finally, toward the end of the night, Jay-Z sang "Where I'm From" from his *In My Lifetime* album. This song contains a lyric about whether Biggie Smalls, Jay-Z, or Nas is the best emcee. After he recited that line, Jay-Z had the DJ stop the record. Was it finally wartime?

Slowly, Jay-Z started talking to the audience. He said that he had planned to declare war but had changed his mind. Instead of war, he said he would be hosting the United Nations. Then, from out of the

**November 21, 2006**

# Jay-Z is a very busy man

From the Pages of
USA TODAY

Jay-Z may be back to rapping, but the president of Def Jam Records still has a record label to run. He is nearing the end of the second year of a three-year deal that runs through January 2008. With nearly 70 releases annually to oversee, it's a full-time job, and he says he still enjoys the challenge.

"It's been great," he says. "The first year we had the No. 2 market share and this year, if everything goes right, we'll have the No. 1. I've had my great successes and I've had my failures, but that's not unlike any other label. We put out so much product, it's unrealistic to believe all of them are going to be successful."

With a roster that includes the likes of superstars Kanye West and Ludacris, and fresh acts such as Rihanna, Young Jeezy and Rick Ross, the label has had plenty of hits. He says helping develop stars out of new artists is one of the rewards of the job. "I love the process," he says. "It's another way of being creative. Especially with a new artist, when somebody walks in and they don't understand what's going on and they are all wide-eyed. Then the next year, they are signing autographs and they're big, too."

darkness, Nas—Jay-Z's archrival—appeared onstage. The audience screamed with excitement.

Several years before, Jay-Z and Nas had hurled insults back and forth on their songs. But this time, there was no war. The two rappers started singing together. They joined forces on "Dead Presidents" and merged it with Nas's 1994 track "The World Is Yours," a song sampled on "Dead Presidents." When the singing was over, the two rivals shook hands to end the concert. The audience gave them a standing ovation. One of the great wars of hip-hop had ended with a peace treaty. Observers called it a classic moment in hip-hop history. The following

One of his biggest coups was signing longtime rival and revered wordsmith Nas whose first Def Jam album, *Hip Hop Is Dead*, is due Dec. 19. Jay Z and Nas staged one of hip-hop's most legendary lyrical beefs for years, but ended it in October 2005 in New Jersey, where they shared the stage together at what was billed as the I Declare War concert. New albums also are coming next month from rising star Jeezy and Wu-Tang Clan founding member Ghostface Killah, who already released the acclaimed *Fishscale* this year.

Not everybody has been happy during his two-year tenure. Rappers LL Cool J, Method Man and DMX (who left the label) have publicly criticized Jay-Z for his handling of their albums. "I try not to take it personally," Jay-Z says.

There is lingering animosity over his 2004 split with longtime partners Damon Dash and Kareem Biggs after they sold their stake in Roc-A-Fella Records to Island Def Jam. In his position as president, Jay-Z continues to run the label. Last year, Jay-Z bought out co-founder Dash's share of their lucrative Rocawear fashion company.

Looking to 2007, he's hoping to line up a star-studded tour that could feature all of Def Jam's major stars. Another priority for him is the revival of Roc-A-Fella, whose latest releases by the likes of Memphis Bleek and the Young Gunz haven't sold well. When he retired, he passed the torch to West as the label's top draw, but no one else on the street-oriented label has made a splash.

"I'm looking for a new guy and some fresh blood to carry the flag," he says. "Kanye did it, but he did it in such a big way. I'm hunting for the new hungry guy to be at the forefront of Roc-A- Fella."

—Steve Jones

year, Jay-Z signed Nas to a record contract at Def Jam.

## Comings and Goings

Jay-Z had said that *The Black Album* would be his last solo album, but by 2006, he was in the studio making a new one. He released this "comeback" album, *Kingdom Come*, in November 2006. The reviewers were not impressed. They said that *Kingdom Come* was boring. They said that Jay-Z's flow wasn't sharp—that he had lost his edge. Despite the criticism, the record still sold well, debuting at No. 1 on the *Billboard* 200.

# Water for Life

In October 2006, Jay-Z took an extraordinary trip. He had traveled the world, giving concerts in Europe, Asia, and elsewhere. But this trip wasn't about music. The journey took Jay-Z to impoverished villages in Angola, a nation in southwestern Africa. Jay-Z had arranged the trip in partnership with MTV and the United Nations (UN). The goal was to call attention to the global water crisis.

According to the UN, more than 1 billion people around the world do not have access to clean drinking water, and more than 2.6 billion people do not have proper sanitation, such as showers, sinks, or toilets. People without clean, running water must sometimes wash in and even drink dirty, germ-infected water. Dirty water spreads serious, sometimes deadly, diseases. The water problem is particularly serious in Africa.

Jay-Z visited Angola twice, and an MTV film crew followed him to document his travels. In a rural village, he hiked a rugged trail with schoolchildren to fetch water from a river. In the town of Luanda, he saw an open sewer running through a city street and saw children playing around the filthy water. Jay-Z found the experience eye-opening and heartbreaking. He hoped the final film, *Diary of Jay-Z: Water for Life* (2006), would help bring about change. At the end of the film, Jay-Z concluded, "So many people that I've seen can't get clean water. It's a crime. I'm on a mission, and I will never forget."

**New knowledge:** Jay-Z performs in Cape Town, South Africa, during a 2006 tour. Around this time, he also visited the nearby country of Angola and learned about water politics.

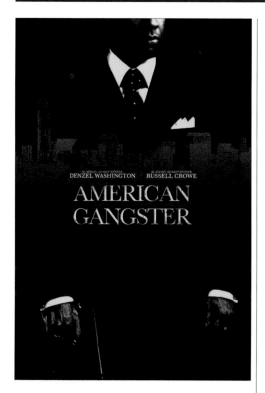

**The outlaw life:** The movie *American Gangster* (2007) reminded Jay-Z of his childhood. Jay-Z wrote a companion album to the film.

Returning to his previous pace of one album per year, Jay-Z followed *Kingdom Come* with *American Gangster* in 2007. The album was a companion piece to the film *American Gangster*, starring Denzel Washington. The film told the story of real-life drug kingpin Frank Lucas. Set in New York in the 1970s, the movie reminded Jay-Z of his father, his uncles, and his own childhood. He could also relate to Washington's outlaw character because he'd lived the outlaw life himself. "It's one of those movies where you champion the bad guy, because the bad guy, he don't seem like a bad guy, and the good guy—I mean the good guys are bad," Jay-Z explained during an interview.

Sean "Diddy" Combs and other producers sampled from Curtis Mayfield, Marvin Gaye, Barry White, and other soul and funk artists to give *American Gangster* a 1970s feel. Many songs revisited the drug-dealing themes of Jay-Z's earlier albums, with the same gritty edge. Unlike *Kingdom Come*, this was classic Jay-Z hip-hop. "This is probably as close as the new Jay-Z will ever come to sounding like the old Jay-Z," wrote a *New York Times* reviewer. "Forget Frank Lucas," gushed *Rolling Stone*, "the real black superhero here is Jay." The album sold more than 425,000 copies in its first week of release and shot to No. 1 on the *Billboard* 200.

Jay-Z was a busy man. He made his own albums, collaborated with other artists, toured, endorsed products, and invested in businesses. In 2007 he sold Rocawear to a company called Iconix Brand Group for $204 million, but he remained with Iconix to promote and manage the business. (Iconix decided to pare down Rocawear to focus on menswear only. It sold off Rocawear's women's, kids', and accessories lines.)

While Jay-Z juggled his many musical and business activities, he continued to serve as president of Def Jam Records. Jay-Z had made some big scores at Def Jam. Under his guidance, producer-turned-rapper Kanye West had become a star. Rihanna had become a pop sensation. Jay-Z had had some disappointments at Def Jam as well. Sales were slow for Freeway, Beanie Sigel, and other acts he had signed to the label.

Jay-Z's employment contract was up for renewal at the end of 2007. He and the bosses at Universal couldn't come to terms, so Jay-Z resigned in late December 2007. "It's time for me to take on some new challenges," he told the press.

**Out and about:** Jay-Z and Beyoncé watch the men's final of the U.S. Open, a tennis competition, in 2011.

# New Alliances

■■■■■

Jay-Z and Beyoncé had always kept their romance quiet. When they decided to get married in early 2008, they hoped to do so out of the public eye. Finally, right before the wedding, the press found out. Reporters learned that the couple had obtained a marriage license at the beginning of April in Scarsdale, New York.

Then, on April 4, reporters saw signs that a party was brewing. Workers had erected a white tent on the roof of a New York building where Jay-Z had a penthouse (top-floor) apartment. Vehicles began delivering flowers, audio equipment, candelabras, and other gear. Beyoncé's parents and the other members of Destiny's Child arrived, as did actor Gwyneth Paltrow and her husband, rock star Chris Martin of Coldplay. A celebrity party was clearly about to begin.

In the end, Jay-Z and Beyoncé managed to keep the event private. Only about thirty guests—plus some servers and other staff—attended the ceremony and the party. Only they

**Star power:** Jay-Z greets Beyoncé and actress friend Gwyneth Paltrow *(right)* after a 2006 concert in London, England. Paltrow and husband Chris Martin attended Jay-Z and Beyoncé's wedding.

knew the details of the wedding. But according to one person in attendance, the decorations included fifty or sixty thousand white orchids from Thailand. Jay-Z's friend DJ Cassidy reportedly spun records. Even after the wedding, Jay-Z and Beyoncé never spoke about it to the press. Finally, a few months later, Beyoncé showed off an 18-karat diamond wedding ring on her finger.

### Rock vs. Hip-Hop?
Jay-Z began another new partnership in early 2008. He joined forces with concert promotion company Live Nation to create a new business called Roc Nation. This would be a record label and much more.

# Another Superstar

Jay-Z's wife, Beyoncé Knowles, was born in Houston, Texas, in 1981. As a child, she loved to sing. At the age of seven, she performed the John Lennon song "Imagine" at a talent contest. The crowd gave her a standing ovation, and the judges named her the winner of the contest. Beyoncé won many more talent shows after that.

Around 1990 Beyoncé and several friends formed a band called Girls Tyme. The girls performed around Houston. They even competed on *Star Search*, a nationally televised talent contest. The group's name and lineup changed over the years. By 1996 it was called Destiny's Child. At this point, the members were Beyoncé, Kelly Rowland, LaTavia Roberson, and LeToya Luckett.

Beyoncé's father quit his job to manage the group. He helped them negotiate a deal with Columbia Records. Their first album, *Destiny's Child*, came out in 1998. Their second album, *The Writing's on the Wall*, was a huge hit. In 2000 *Destiny's Child* went through another lineup change. It became a trio consisting of Beyoncé, Kelly Rowland, and Michelle Williams.

In 2001 Beyoncé moved into acting. She appeared with Mike Myers in the comedy *Austin Powers in Goldmember*. The next year she collaborated with Jay-Z on the song "'03 Bonnie & Clyde." Beyoncé released her first solo album, *Dangerously in Love*, in 2003. The album won five Grammy Awards. She released one more record with Destiny's Child in 2004.

Beyoncé split her time between music and several other projects. In 2005 she and her mother launched a high-end clothing line called Deréon. She released the album *B'Day* in 2006. The same year, Beyoncé starred in *Dreamgirls*, a movie about three female soul singers in the early 1960s. In 2008 Beyoncé married Jay-Z. She also starred in the movie *Cadillac Records*, in which she played legendary gospel and R & B singer Etta James.

Beyoncé released her third album, *I Am . . . Sasha Fierce*, in 2009. At the Grammy Awards in February 2010, she took home six trophies—the most ever for a female artist. She released her fourth record, *4*, in 2011.

**Destined for fame:** Beyoncé sings at the Grammy Awards in 2010.

In addition to producing and distributing music, the company would also handle the management, tours, film and TV appearances, and business ventures of its artists. Jay-Z would put out his new records through Roc Nation instead of Def Jam. He would also sign new artists to the label.

After the Roc Nation deal was inked, Jay-Z went back into the studio. He also hit the road. He signed on to appear at the Glastonbury Festival, a famous outdoor rock 'n' roll festival in the United Kingdom. When Noel Gallagher of the British rock band Oasis heard that Jay-Z would be the lead act at Glastonbury, he protested. "I'm not having hip-hop at Glastonbury," he said. "It's wrong."

Gallagher's remarks raised eyebrows. What did he have against hip-hop? Observers noted that a diverse group of musicians had played at Glastonbury over the years. They included soul singers, reggae bands, and funk bands. Maybe hip-hop, with its harsh lyrics and angry beats, somehow offended Gallagher. But Jay-Z was confident that hip-hop had earned its rightful place alongside rock music. "Kids today have a mix of songs from all over the place in their iPods," he said. "There is no rock music with walls around it."

The dustup with Gallagher quickly blew over, and 180,000 people came to see Jay-Z's show at Glastonbury. But Jay-Z couldn't pass up the chance to make a little dig

**Controversy:** Noel Gallagher, known for his work with the band Oasis, wasn't happy to hear that Jay-Z was headlining England's Glastonbury Festival in 2008.

at Gallagher. To kick off his performance, he walked out onstage with an electric guitar slung around his neck like a true rock star. Then he jokingly launched into Oasis's hit song "Wonderwall." The audience laughed and happily sang along. Later that evening, when Jay-Z sang "99 Problems," the audience joined in on that song too. "To the crowd, it wasn't rock and rap or a battle of genres," Jay-Z wrote later. "It was music."

**Last laugh:** Jay-Z leads the crowd in a jokey version of the Oasis song "Wonderwall" while onstage at Glastonbury.

## The Oval Office

In 2005 Jay-Z had bought partial ownership in a New York City restaurant, the Spotted Pig. Other musicians, including the Irish rock star Bono (Paul Hewson), also had ownership shares. Jay-Z was in the Spotted Pig one night in 2008 when Bono brought former U.S. president Bill Clinton to the restaurant. Bono introduced Clinton to Jay-Z, and the three men hung out, telling jokes and talking about music.

Jay-Z enjoyed meeting Bill Clinton, but he was far more excited that year to meet a different politician: Barack Obama. Obama, an African American senator from Illinois, was trying to win the Democratic presidential nomination. (His main opponent was Bill Clinton's wife, Hillary.)

June 28, 2011

# Beyoncé vulnerable in album "4"

From the Pages of
USA TODAY
Last year, Beyoncé announced that she was done with the alter ego she created to distinguish her aggressive stage persona from her shyer real-life personality on 2008's *I Am . . . Sasha Fierce*. And in fact, there are only traces of Sasha on the R&B superstar's new album, *4*, which exposes a much more vulnerable side.

The first half is filled with sweeping, emotional ballads that find her pining for love that is distant, taking comfort in one that's close, and trying to hold on when things get shaky. She opens with the tender "1+1," which promises undying love, then patiently lets her paramour know "I Care," even if he no longer does.

But in typical Beyoncé fashion, she lets a bit of steel creep in with the sensitivity, just to be sure it's not mistaken for weakness. On current single "Best Thing I Never Had," for example, she kisses off an arrogant guy.

A battalion of name producers and songwriters (The-Dream, Babyface, Kanye West, Jeff Bhasker, Ryan Tedder, Diane Warren) have been enlisted, and they generally keep the tracks spare enough so as to not get in the way of the singer's voice, which is stronger and more assured than ever. There are some purely fun elements sprinkled in, such as the swaggering "Countdown," in which she boasts of all the ways her guy is lucky to have her, and the West-produced "Party," which features an always welcome rhyme from the seldom-heard Andre 3000.

At 29, the still-in-her-prime Beyoncé seems a little young to be worrying about her legacy, as she does on the Warren power ballad "I Was Here." But she puts so much feeling into it that it winds up being the album's most moving song.

Compared with Beyoncé's three previous albums, which arrived on a wave of hit singles, the release of *4* seems relatively quiet. Neither lead single "Run the World (Girls)" nor "Best Thing I Never Had" has caught fire on the charts.

But after *Fierce*'s duality, Beyoncé does not seem to need to make a cutting-edge statement. This time, she's content to stay in her comfort zone.

—Steve Jones

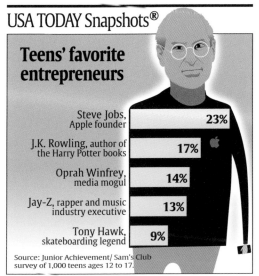

USA TODAY Snapshots®

**Teens' favorite entrepreneurs**

| | |
|---|---|
| Steve Jobs, Apple founder | 23% |
| J.K. Rowling, author of the Harry Potter books | 17% |
| Oprah Winfrey, media mogul | 14% |
| Jay-Z, rapper and music industry executive | 13% |
| Tony Hawk, skateboarding legend | 9% |

Source: Junior Achievement/ Sam's Club survey of 1,000 teens ages 12 to 17.

By Jae Yang and Alejandro Gonzalez, USA TODAY, 2010

Someone on Obama's staff was a big Jay-Z fan, and he arranged for the rapper and the candidate to meet. Obama reportedly wanted to ask Jay-Z, "What's going on in America?"

Jay-Z was eager to talk politics. He was upset about the George W. Bush administration and its response to Hurricane Katrina. He was upset about Bush's decision to send U.S. troops into the country of Iraq in 2003. He talked to Obama about these issues and much more. Jay-Z remembers that Obama "asked question after

**Jay's candidate:** Barack Obama greets supporters in Saint Louis, Missouri, during his 2008 campaign for president. At the time, Obama was serving as a U.S. senator from Illinois.

question, about music, about where I'm from, about what people in my circle—not the circle of wealthy entertainers, but the wider circle that reaches out to my fans and all the way back to Marcy—were thinking and concerned about politically. He listened. It was extraordinary."

Obama was equally impressed with Jay-Z. He told reporters that he had Jay-Z's music on his iPod. At a press conference, Obama talked about the mudslinging that goes on in political campaigns. "When you're running for the presidency, then you've got to expect it," Obama said, "and you've just got to, kind of . . ." At that point, Obama stopped talking and started brushing his shoulder with his fingers. The audience cheered and laughed. They realized that Obama was referencing a Jay-Z song, "Dirt Off Your Shoulder" from *The Black Album*. The message was: don't let your opponents get you down or get under your skin.

**Hip-hop for Obama:** Jay-Z takes part in a campaign rally for Barack Obama, along with stars such as Sean Combs *(far left)* and Mary J. Blige *(second from right)*.

**Time to celebrate:** Beyoncé and Jay-Z attend the presidential inauguration of Barack Obama in Washington, D.C., on January 20, 2009.

Obama knew that a lot of Jay-Z's listeners were likely to vote for a young, hip, African American candidate—someone hip-hop fans could relate to. So after Obama won the Democratic nomination in August, he asked Jay-Z to help with the campaign. Jay-Z was thrilled to do his part to elect the first African American president. Along with Mary J. Blige, Diddy, and others, he held a series of free concerts all around the United States. At the concerts, the performers encouraged people who had not already done so to register to vote—and encouraged them to vote for Barack Obama.

In November Obama won the election, beating the Republican candidate John McCain by a large margin. To celebrate, Jay-Z rapped over a remix of Young Jeezy's song "My President (Is Black)." Jay-Z's lyrics referenced Rosa Parks and Martin Luther King Jr., pioneers in the fight for civil rights for African Americans.

In January 2009, Jay-Z and Beyoncé flew to Washington, D.C., to see Obama inaugurated (sworn in) as the forty-fourth president of the United States. The day before the inauguration, Beyoncé performed at the Lincoln Memorial. At the Inaugural Ball, she sang for the new president and his wife, Michelle. She chose the song "At Last," made famous in the 1960s by gospel and R & B singer Etta James.

The night after the inauguration, Jay-Z gave a concert for thousands of volunteers who had worked on the Obama campaign. He shouted to the audience, "If you're proud to be an American, put your hands up now!"

# IN F⊙CUS

## You Gotta Have Art

Jay-Z is an art lover. One of his favorite painters is Jean-Michel Basquiat, an African American artist who died in 1988. Much like hip-hop, Basquiat's work captures the energy of urban black life. His paintings are chaotic and colorful, with lots of words scribbled around the images. Works by Basquiat are highly valued, selling for millions of dollars. Jay-Z owns several of Basquiat's paintings. He also owns works by other famous artists, including Andy Warhol, a pioneering pop artist of the 1960s.

**Powerful visions:** Jay-Z collects artwork by Jean-Michel Basquiat, seen here in 1983. Basquiat is a legendary African American painter.

**At last:** Beyoncé sings for President Barack Obama and First Lady Michelle Obama during the Neighborhood Inaugural Ball in 2009.

Jay-Z wrote later about the importance of having a black president: "This was big. This was a chance [for African Americans] to go from centuries of invisibility to the most visible position in the entire world. He [Obama] could, through sheer symbolism ... change the lives of millions of black kids who now saw something different to aspire to."

**Root for the home team:** Jay-Z and Alicia Keys perform "Empire State of Mind" for the New York Yankees during the 2009 Major League Baseball playoffs.

# Empire

Jay-Z released his eleventh album, *The Blueprint 3*, in 2009. It was his first album on the new Roc Nation label. It debuted at No. 1 on the *Billboard* charts and went platinum within a month.

The album contained a number of hit tracks. The song "D.O.A. (Death of Auto-Tune)" took a swipe at rappers who use Auto-Tune, a computer program, to improve and sometimes distort their singing voices. "Run This Town" was an edgy, boastful song with guest raps by Kanye West and vocals by Rihanna. But by far the biggest hit off *The Blueprint 3* was "Empire State of Mind," with vocals by Alicia Keys.

New York is nicknamed the Empire State, and this song was a tribute to the state's biggest city, New York City. As Jay-Z rapped on "Empire State," he rattled off names of city neighborhoods and streets—places he had lived when he was poor and when he was rich. He rapped about New York Knicks basketball games and New York Yankee baseball games, the Statue of Liberty, and the city's diverse ethnic mix. On the chorus, Alicia Keys sang about the city as a place where people can reach their dreams.

*The Blueprint 3* came out in September 2009. By October the New York Yankees were in the Major League Baseball playoffs, working their way toward a World Series championship. "Empire State of Mind" became the unofficial anthem of the Yankees' postseason. Jay-Z performed the song in Yankee Stadium before one World Series game.

**Game six:** The New York Yankees celebrate their World Series victory against the Philadelphia Phillies on November 4, 2009. Jay-Z's "Empire State of Mind" was the soundtrack to the big win.

After the Yankees won the championship, "Empire State of Mind" played through giant loudspeakers at the victory parade.

## Home and Away

Jay-Z followed up *The Blueprint 3* with his Blueprint 3 Tour. The trip took him to sixty-two cities. Back home in New York, he stayed busy in the studio. He also continued to run Rocawear. In the company's headquarters, in a skyscraper in New York City's garment district, Jay-Z worked in a big thirty-ninth-floor office, with views across the East River. The walls were decorated with pictures of people Jay-Z admired:

# IN FOCUS

## Bigger Than Elvis

With the release of *American Gangster* in 2007, Jay-Z tied rock 'n' roll legend Elvis Presley for the most No. 1 albums of all time—ten. Then *The Blueprint 3* went to No. 1, putting Jay-Z ahead of Presley.

Except for Jay-Z's first two albums, *Reasonable Doubt* and *In My Lifetime...Vol. 1*, all of Jay-Z's solo records have hit the No. 1 spot. He also had No. 1 albums with R. Kelly (*Unfinished Business*) and with Linkin Park (*Collision Course*). His 2011 collaboration with Kanye West, *Watch the Throne*, also went to No. 1, giving Jay-Z a total of twelve No. 1 albums.

**Hit maker:** Elvis Presley, seen here in 1959, has been called the King of Rock 'n' Roll.

## USA TODAY Snapshots®

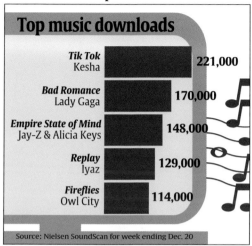

**Top music downloads**

*Tik Tok*
Kesha — 221,000

*Bad Romance*
Lady Gaga — 170,000

*Empire State of Mind*
Jay-Z & Alicia Keys — 148,000

*Replay*
Iyaz — 129,000

*Fireflies*
Owl City — 114,000

Source: Nielsen SoundScan for week ending Dec. 20

By Steve Jones and Veronica Salazar, USA TODAY, 2009

boxer Muhammad Ali, pretending to knock out all the Beatles with one punch; soul singer Ray Charles; twentieth-century entertainers Frank Sinatra, Dean Martin, and Sammy Davis Jr.; and painter Jean-Michel Basquiat.

Between his job at Rocawear and his income from tours and music sales, Jay-Z took home an estimated $82 million a year. His wealth was said to be near $500 million. He used some of that money to invest in new business ventures. He also gave generously to charity.

When Hurricane Katrina had flooded New Orleans in 2005, Jay-Z had given money to help the victims—but had not given his time or talent. When a massive earthquake hit the Caribbean nation of Haiti in January 2010, killing 150,000 and leaving 1.5 million homeless, Jay-Z wanted to give more than just money. He joined a telethon (televised fund-raiser) to help the victims. At the event, held on January 22, Jay-Z, Bono, and Rihanna performed a new song, "Stranded (Haiti Mon Amour)." Other performers sang or staffed telephone lines to collect donations from viewers. Altogether, the telethon raised $57 million for victims of the earthquake.

### Words from the Throne

In 2003 Jay-Z had worked with hip-hop journalist Dream Hampton to write his biography. After most of the writing was complete, however, Jay-Z decided he wasn't comfortable publishing intimate details about

**Giving back:** Bono *(left)*, Jay-Z, and Rihanna *(right)* perform "Stranded (Haiti Mon Amour)" in January of 2010. The artists joined together at a benefit for victims of an earthquake that struck the island nation of Haiti.

his life for all to see. The project, titled *The Black Book*, was canceled. But by 2010, Jay-Z was finally ready to tell his story. He wrote a new book, *Decoded*, once again working with Dream Hampton. This book not only explored Jay-Z's life but also analyzed many of his songs. In the book, Jay-Z takes readers line by line through thirty-six songs and explains the slang, stories, and hidden meanings inside the lyrics.

Released in November 2010, *Decoded* garnered great praise. It is a "truly magnificent book, soul-searching, deeply honest, candid, highly poetic," said Paul Holdengräber, director of public programs at the New York Public Library. Jay-Z was especially thrilled when kids wrote to him, saying, "This is the first book I've ever read all the way through." He elaborated, "For all the other accolades [praise] the book received, the thing that makes me happiest is knowing that it's working as a gateway drug for kids to get into reading and into thinking about new ways to use their own voices and experiences."

After releasing *Decoded*, Jay-Z teamed up with his good friend Kanye West to create a new collaborative album, *Watch the Throne*. Many of the tracks dealt with power, fame, riches, and success—topics that both Jay-Z and Kanye had come to know well. Guest artists on the album included Frank Ocean, Beyoncé, and Mr Hudson. Kanye did much of the production work. Released in August 2011, the album was yet another platinum-level success for Jay-Z.

## Baby Bump

Jay-Z and Kanye went on tour to promote *Watch the Throne* in the fall of 2011. But Jay-Z had much more on his mind than music that fall.

**Kings:** Kanye West *(left)* and Jay-Z recorded the album *Watch the Throne* in 2011 and then toured together to support the release.

**November 16, 2010**

# Jay-Z decodes his life story

From the Pages of
USA TODAY

As anyone who has followed Jay-Z's career knows, the superstar born Shawn Corey Carter has long defied anyone who tried to pigeonhole him. Since rising to fame as a rapper in the late '90s, Jay-Z, 40, also has racked up credits as a record company CEO, fashion mogul, philanthropist and co- or part owner of properties ranging from the 40/40 Club chain to the NBA's New Jersey Nets.

Now Jay-Z is adding another title to his resume: author. Today sees the release of *Decoded*, a book that uses 36 of his songs to examine both his own journey and that of hip-hop. Each chapter is accompanied by extensively annotated lyrics, plus photos and illustrations of icons who have informed his work. There are personal recollections, tributes to other artists and political and social commentary. "I didn't want it to be this self-aggrandizing

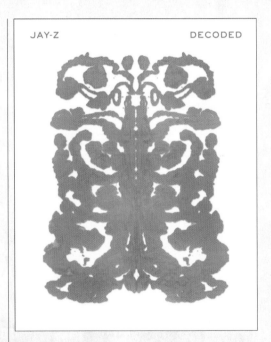

JAY-Z                    DECODED

**Author:** Jay-Z's book *Decoded (cover above)*, released in 2011, took readers through some of his lyrics and shared with them his life story.

book about how I put triple and quadruple metaphors together," he says.

Nor did he want to release a standard celebrity autobiography. He had worked on something closer to that in recent years, an uncompleted project called *The Black Book*. Instead of focusing on his own story, "I wanted to tell the story of a generation, and to make the case that rap is beautiful poetry."

Former *Vibe* editor Alan Light isn't surprised that Jay-Z would choose not to deliver a straight memoir. "As with other media, he's not taking the expected route. It's another example of his creative ambition."

*Decoded* doesn't shy away from darker aspects of Jay-Z's past, such as how he dealt drugs while coming of age in Brooklyn's Marcy Projects. "My life after childhood has two main stories: the story of the hustler and the story of the rapper, and the two overlap as much as they diverge," he writes. "I'm not ashamed of what I did [drug dealing]—it was bad, but you have to put it in context." That context includes a father who left the family when Jay-Z was about 9. The rapper reconciled with his dad before Adnis Reeves' death in 2003.

For all his celebrated business acumen, Jay-Z insists he is far more passionate about art than business. "If somebody tells me we did a deal for X amount of money, I'm like, 'OK, good job.'" On the other hand, when he learned that Andy Warhol's estate had approved the use of his painting *Rorschach* for the cover of *Decoded*, "I was jumping up and down."

Not that he seems more blasé about corporate pursuits. Asked about his goals, Jay-Z says, "I want to build Roc Nation into the biggest entertainment company in the world." Founded with showbiz behemoth Live Nation in 2008, the multimedia firm boasts a roster of clients ranging from Rihanna to rising child star Willow Smith.

Jay-Z['s] ambitions [also] include fatherhood. "I grew up with people in my house all the time. . . . So family is important to me. But I don't rush anything; everything happens in time."

Living in the moment is, in fact, a huge part of Jay-Z's personal and creative philosophy. "I just had a birthday party for my grandmother, her 85th," he says. "It was in Brooklyn, at this warehouse overlooking the Statue of Liberty. There was a jazz player on the balcony, and we had drinks outside before we went in for dinner and dancing. To me, that was a perfect celebration of life. We all need more of that."

Jay-Z gestures outside an enormous window, to the sun beaming down on Manhattan. "Look how beautiful it is right now. You can't take things like that for granted."

—Elysa Gardner

Beyoncé was pregnant. Reporters first noticed her "baby bump" in August, at the MTV Video Music Awards. Beyoncé and Jay-Z had always kept their life together private, but Beyoncé couldn't hide her expanding waistline. She confirmed that she was expecting a baby in early 2012.

As their baby's due date drew near, Beyoncé and Jay-Z were more mindful of their privacy than ever. They didn't want reporters hounding them at the hospital when the baby arrived. They wanted complete security and peace, so they rented out a section of New York's Lenox Hill Hospital ahead of time. The area was off-limits to everyone but the couple's family and medical staff. When it was time for the delivery, security guards made sure that no unauthorized people got anywhere near Jay-Z, Beyoncé, or the new baby. On January 7, Beyoncé gave birth to a girl, Blue Ivy Carter.

**New baby:** Beyoncé leaves a New York City store while holding Blue Ivy Carter in July 2012.

In a statement released to the press, Jay-Z and Beyoncé said, "We are happy to announce the arrival of our beautiful daughter, Blue Ivy Carter. . . . Her birth was emotional and extremely peaceful, we are in heaven. . . . It was the best experience of both of our lives." Jay-Z wrote a song for his daughter

## A Stand for Gay Rights

In May 2012, President Barack Obama came out in favor of gay marriage. This was a controversial stance, since many Americans believe that same-sex couples shouldn't be allowed to marry. After Obama's announcement, a reporter asked Jay-Z whether he agreed with the president. Jay-Z said that he did. He said that discrimination against gay people "is no different than discriminating against blacks. It's discrimination plain and simple." The reporter noted that the president's stance was risky, because it might cost him votes in the 2012 presidential election. "It's really not about votes," Jay-Z said. "It's about people. Whether it costs him votes or not, it's the right thing to do."

called "Glory." In it, he said she was the most beautiful little girl in the world.

### Onward

Jay-Z took a short break from performing after Blue Ivy was born. Then he jumped back into the spotlight. On February 6 and 7, he gave two concerts at swanky Carnegie Hall in New York City to raise money for the United Way and the Shawn Carter Scholarship Foundation. These were no casual, come-as-you-are hip-hop shows. Tickets cost $300 and up. When the show opened, Jay-Z came onstage in a white tuxedo and a black bow tie, with a diamond pin in his lapel. The audience also came dressed to the hilt. Women wore elegant gowns and high-heeled shoes. Men wore suits and tuxedos.

But once the music started and the raucous sound of hip-hop took over the auditorium, everyone cut loose. Jay-Z sang many of his chart-topping hits: "Izzo (H.O.V.A.)," "Hard Knock Life (Ghetto Anthem),"

"Dirt Off Your Shoulder," "99 Problems," and others. He brought in Alicia Keys to join him on "Empire State of Mind" and Nas to rap on "If I Ruled the World." Toward the end of the night, Jay-Z sang "Glory," his tribute to his new daughter.

A few months later, Jay-Z was back on the road, touring Europe with Kanye West. They sang in London, England; Zurich, Switzerland; Oslo, Norway; Paris, France; Frankfurt, Germany; and other European cities. Everywhere they went, audiences went crazy. People held up their hands to make Jay-Z's dynasty symbol. They cheered, shouted, and sang along. The crowds were filled with people of every age, every background, and every color.

In the course of his career, Jay-Z had brought rap music from the streets of Brooklyn to the finest concert halls in the world. In the process, he had broken down barriers. "I think if you make great music,

**Another level:** Jay-Z raps from the balcony at New York City's Carnegie Hall in February 2012.

# IN F⬤CUS

## Challenges for Damon Dash

Although Damon Dash split with Roc-A-Fella Records and Def Jam in 2004, he did not exit the music business. Instead, Dash launched the Damon Dash Music Group in 2006. He also formed a business called DD172. Based in the Tribeca neighborhood of New York, DD172 was a combination art gallery, rehearsal space, nightclub, and record label. Dash's businesses did not flourish, however. Neighbors complained about the noise coming from the DD172 building. In 2011 city officials shut the space down. Dash also found himself in legal trouble. In 2012 the rapper Curren$y sued him for $1.5 million, claiming that Dash released two of his albums illegally. Dash and his employees denied the claim.

it's ageless, it's colorless, it doesn't have a genre, it doesn't have a gender, male and female like it, black and white like it, young and old like it," Jay-Z says.

What will Jay-Z do next? Will he ever stop making music? It seems unlikely. As he wrote in *Decoded*, "There have been times in my life when I've tried to put [rapping] to the side—when I was a kid, so I could focus on hustling on the streets, and when I was an adult, so I could focus on hustling in the boardroom—but the words kept coming. They're still coming and will probably never stop."

## TIMELINE

1969    Jay-Z (real name Shawn Corey Carter) is born in Brooklyn, New York.

1975    Jay-Z's family moves to the Marcy Houses, a development in Brooklyn for low-income people.

ca. 1981    Jay-Z's parents divorce. His father leaves the family home.

ca. 1985    Jay-Z begins selling crack cocaine in Trenton, New Jersey.

1987    Jay-Z and Jaz-O record a track on a mixtape with Big Daddy Kane.

1988    Jay-Z accompanies Jaz-O to London, England, where Jaz-O cuts a record with the EMI label.

1989    Jay-Z goes on tour with Big Daddy Kane and other rappers.

1993    Jay-Z guest raps on Big Daddy Kane's *Daddy's Home* album.

1994    Jay-Z, Damon Dash, and Kareem "Biggs" Burke decide to form Roc-A-Fella Records.

1996    Roc-A-Fella releases its first album, *Reasonable Doubt*. Def Jam buys 33 percent of Roc-A-Fella Records.

1997    Jay-Z releases *In My Lifetime, Vol. 1*. Biggie Smalls is killed in a drive-by shooting in Los Angeles.

1998    Jay-Z releases *Vol. 2 . . . Hard Knock Life*. Roc-A-Fella Films releases *Streets Is Watching*.

1999    Roc-A-Fella Films produces *Backstage*, a documentary about the Hard Knock Life Tour. Roc-A-Fella Records launches a clothing company called Rocawear. Jay-Z releases *Vol. 3 . . . The Life and Times of S. Carter*.

2000    Jay-Z releases *The Dynasty: Roc La Familia*.

2001    Jay-Z releases *The Blueprint*.

2002    Jay-Z establishes the Shawn Carter Scholarship Foundation to help send low-income students to college. He releases *The Blueprint 2: The Gift and the Curse*. He also begins dating singer Beyoncé Knowles.

**In charge:** Jay-Z sports a Rocawear T-shirt.

2003   Jay-Z reconciles with his father, A. J. Carter. A.J. dies of liver disease. Reebok launches its S. Carter sneaker collection. Jay-Z and two business partners open the 40/40 Club, a sports bar. He also releases *The Black Album* and then holds a "retirement" concert at Madison Square Garden in New York City.

2004   Jay-Z records *Collision Course* with Linkin Park and *Unfinished Business* with R. Kelly. He buys a stake in the New Jersey (later Brooklyn) Nets basketball team. Def Jam buys the remaining share of Roc-A-Fella Records.

2005   Jay-Z becomes president of Def Jam Records. He reconciles with the rapper Nas at the I Declare War concert.

2006   Jay-Z travels to Angola, a nation in Africa, to bring attention to the world water crisis. He releases *Kingdom Come*.

2007   Jay-Z releases *American Gangster*. He sells Rocawear to the Iconix Brand Group. He also resigns from Def Jam.

2008   Jay-Z and Beyoncé get married. He and Live Nation create a new music label and management business, Roc Nation. He sings at the Glastonbury music festival in the United Kingdom. He also meets former president Bill Clinton and presidential candidate Barack Obama and then performs free concerts to support the Obama campaign.

**Red carpet:** Jay-Z and Beyoncé attend the 2005 Academy Awards in Hollywood, California.

2009    Jay-Z and Beyoncé perform at presidential inauguration events in Washington, D.C. He releases *The Blueprint 3*.

2010    Jay-Z performs at a telethon to raise money for Haitian earthquake victims. He publishes *Decoded*, a book about his life and music.

2011    Jay-Z and Kanye West release *Watch the Throne*.

2012    Beyoncé gives birth to a daughter, Blue Ivy Carter. Jay-Z performs at Carnegie Hall.

**album:** a collection of musical works, released as a group on CD, vinyl record, or online

**battle:** a contest between two rappers in which they take turns insulting, or "dissing," each other in rhyme form. An emcee wins a battle not only through skilled rhyming but also by having the cleverest jokes and insults.

**beat:** the background music on a hip-hop track. The producer creates the beat using drum machines, synthesizers, and other equipment, along with samples and loops.

**cipher:** a crowd that encircles a rapper or a battle between rappers

**collaborator:** someone who contributes to a project, such as a song or an album

**DJ:** a musician who uses record albums and a turntable to create new sounds or play beats for rappers; also known as a disc jockey.

**emcee:** another name for a rapper. The name comes from MC, short for master of ceremonies.

**flow:** the rhymes recited by a rapper, usually along with a background beat

**freestyle:** to rap without having written down or memorized rhymes beforehand. Freestyling rappers come up with rhymes on the spur of the moment.

**hip-hop:** a form of music that combines rapped lyrics with instrumental music. Hip-hop also refers to the culture surrounding this music.

**hook:** a memorable instrumental part or vocal part that repeats throughout a song

**hustle:** to work hard, especially at an illegal activity

**mixtape:** a collection of songs that an artist releases separately from an album, often without the help of a record company. While an album will have original beats and production, many mixtapes use beats from other records and hit songs.

**R & B:** rhythm and blues is a form of music that originated in the middle of the twentieth century. R & B is danceable music that borrows from African American blues and gospel music traditions.

**rap:** rhythmic chanting and rhyming, often accompanied by a background beat

**sample:** to take a piece of recorded music from another artist and reuse it as a part of a song's beat or hook. *Sample* is also used to describe the sound that is borrowed for a new song.

**track:** a single recorded song or other piece of music

## DISCOGRAPHY

### SOLO ALBUMS
***Reasonable Doubt***
**Label:** Roc-A-Fella Records
**Released:** 1996

***In My Lifetime, Vol. 1***
**Label:** Roc-A-Fella/Def Jam
**Released:** 1997

***Vol. 2 . . . Hard Knock Life***
**Label:** Roc-A-Fella/Def Jam
**Released:** 1998

***Vol. 3 . . . Life and Times of S. Carter***
**Label:** Roc-A-Fella/Def Jam
**Released:** 1999

***The Dynasty: Roc La Familia***
**Label:** Roc-A-Fella/Def Jam
**Released:** 2000

***The Blueprint***
**Label:** Roc-A-Fella/Def Jam
**Released:** 2001

***The Blueprint 2: The Gift and the Curse***
**Label:** Roc-A-Fella/Def Jam
**Released:** 2002

***The Black Album***
**Label:** Roc-A-Fella/Def Jam
**Released:** 2003

***Kingdom Come***
**Label:** Roc-A-Fella/Def Jam
**Released:** 2006

*American Gangster*
**Label:** Roc-A-Fella/Def Jam
**Released:** 2007

*The Blueprint 3*
**Label:** Roc Nation
**Released:** 2009

COLLABORATIONS
*The Best of Both Worlds* [with R. Kelly]
**Label:** Roc-A-Fella/Def Jam
**Released:** 2002

*Unfinished Business* [with R. Kelly]
**Label:** Roc-A-Fella/Def Jam
**Released:** 2004

*Collision Course* [with Linkin Park]
**Label:** Roc-A-Fella/Def Jam and Warner Brothers
**Released:** 2004

*Watch the Throne* [with Kanye West]
**Label:** Roc-A-Fella/Def Jam and Roc Nation
**Released:** 2011

## SOURCE NOTES

6  *O, the Oprah Magazine*, "Oprah Talks to Jay-Z." October 2009, http://www.oprah.com/omagazine/Oprah-Interviews-Jay-Z-October-2009-Issue-of-O-Magazine (April 26, 2012).

9  New York Public Library, "Decoded: Jay-Z in Conversation with Cornel West," *FORA.tv*, November 15, 2010, http://fora.tv/2010/11/15/Decoded_Jay-Z_in_Conversation_with_Cornel_West#fullprogram (May 19, 2012).

13  Jay-Z, *Decoded* (New York: Spiegel & Grau, 2011), 4.

13  Ibid., 5.

13  New York Public Library, "Decoded: Jay-Z in Conversation with Cornel West."

13  Ibid.

15  Touré, "The Book of Jay," *Rolling Stone*, December 15, 2005, 89.

15  Jay-Z, *Decoded*, 5.

17  Alex Pappademas, "Jay-Z: King," *GQ*, November 2011, http://www.gq.com/moty/2011/jay-z-gq-men-of-the-year-issue (April 27, 2012).

18  Richard Harrington, "Jay-Z's Rhymes of Passion," *Washington Post*, January 2, 2000, http://www.washingtonpost.com/wp-srv/WPcap/2000-01/02/058r-010200-idx.html (May 5, 2012).

18  Zach O'Malley Greenberg, *Empire State of Mind: How Jay-Z Went from Street Corner to Corner Office* (New York: Portfolio, 2011), 15.

19  Jay-Z, *Decoded*, 7.

19  Greenberg, *Empire State of Mind*, 12.

21  Jay-Z, *Decoded*, 75.

22  *O, the Oprah Magazine*, "Oprah Talks to Jay-Z."

27  Ibid.

27  Marshall Fine, "The Music Mogul," *Cigar Aficionado*, May–June 2009, http://www.cigaraficionado.com/webfeatures/show/id/6238/p/1 (May 17, 2012).

29  Jay-Z, *Decoded*, 246.

30  Charlie Rose, "A Conversation with Rapper and Entrepreneur Jay-Z, *Charlie Rose*, October 27, 2004, http://www.charlierose.com/view/interview/1211 (May 19, 2012).

32  Jay-Z, *Decoded*, 251.

32  Fine, "Music Mogul."

34–35  Ifihavent, "Classic Reviews: Reasonable Doubt in the Source (1996),

*ifihavent.wordpress.com*, December 2, 2008, http://ifihavent
.wordpress.com/2008/12/02/classic-reviews-reasonable-doubt-in-
the-source-1996 (May 19, 2012).

38 Jay-Z, *Decoded*, 12.

39 eNotes, "Jay-Z," *eNotes.com*, 2012, http://www.enotes.com/jay-z-
reference/jay-z (May 19, 2012).

45 Kris Ex, "Jay-Z, Vol. 3 Life and Times of S. Carter," *Rolling Stone*,
February 3, 2000, http://www.rollingstone.com/music/albumreviews
/vol-3-life-and-times-of-s-carter-20000203#ixzz1uURrq5py (May
19, 2012).

47 eNotes, "Jay-Z."

49 Jason Birchmeier, "The Blueprint," *All Music*, 2012, http://www
.allmusic.com/album/the-blueprint-r549749/review (May 19, 2012).

53 Touré, "Book of Jay," 94.

57 Greenberg, *Empire State of Mind*, 83.

59 Touré, "Book of Jay," 93.

63 Ibid., 89.

63 Ibid.

65–66 Jay-Z, *Decoded*, 219–220.

70 Alexandra Olson, "Jay-Z's Journey to Africa," *CBS News*, February 11,
2009, http://www.cbsnews.com/2100-207_162-2195007.html (May
19, 2012).

71 Fresh Air, "Jay-Z: The Fresh Air Interview," *NPR Music*, November 16,
2012, http://www.npr.org/2010/11/16/131334322/the-fresh-air-
interview-jay-z-decoded (May 19, 2012).

71 Kelefa Sanneh, "Jay-Z Finds Himself at the Movies," *New York Times*,
November 5, 2007, http://www.nytimes.com/2007/11/05/arts
/music/05jayz.html?pagewanted=all (May 19, 2012).

71 Rob Sheffield, "Jay-Z, American Gangster," *Rolling Stone Reviews*,
November 15, 2007, http://www.rollingstone.com/music
/albumreviews/american-gangster-20071115 (May 19, 2012).

72 Jeff Leeds, "Jay-Z to Quit His Day Job as President of Def Jam, *New
York Times*, December 25, 2007, http://www.nytimes
.com/2007/12/25/business/25music.html (May 19, 2012).

76 Rosie Swash, "Gallagher Brands Jay-Z 'Wrong for Glasto'," *Guardian*,
April 14, 2008, http://www.guardian.co.uk/music/2008/apr/14/jayz
.urban (May 19, 2012).

76 Jay-Z, *Decoded*, 163.

77   Ibid.

79   Lisa Taddeo, "Jay-Z: It Takes a Harmless, Hand-Built Gangster to Run This Town," *Esquire*, February 2010, http://www.esquire.com /features/people-who-matter-2010/jay-z-business-0210 (May 4, 2012).

80   Jay-Z, *Decoded*, 168.

80   "Obama Brushes the Dirt Off," YouTube video, 0:60, from CNN footage and Jay-Z music, posted by ninja5py, April 17, 2008, http:// www.youtube.com/watch?v=zZJex9Ge2-Q (May 19, 2012).

82   Jay-Z, *Decoded*, 153.

83   Ibid., 168.

88   New York Public Library, "Decoded."

88–89 Jay-Z, *Decoded*, 311.

92   Beyoncé, "Joint Statement from Beyoncé and Jay-Z," Beyoncé Online, January 9, 2012, http://www.beyonceonline.com/us/news/joint-statement-beyonc%C3%A9-jay-z%E2%80%A6 (May 19, 2012).

93   *Daily Beast*, "Jay-Z Backs Obama on Gay Marriage," May 15, 2012, http://www.thedailybeast.com/cheats/2012/05/15/jay-z-backs-obama-on-gay-marriage.html (June 11, 2012).

94–95 Emmanuel Brown, "NY-Z: Jay-Z," *Vimeo*, 2012, http://vimeo .com/10372136 (May 19, 2012).

95   Jay-Z, *Decoded*, 308.

## SELECTED BIBLIOGRAPHY

Fine, Marshall. "The Music Mogul." *Cigar Aficionado*, May–June 2009. 2012. http://www.cigaraficionado.com/webfeatures/show/id/6238/p/1 (May 17, 2012).

Greenberg, Zach O'Malley. *Empire State of Mind: How Jay-Z Went from Street Corner to Corner Office*. New York: Portfolio, 2011.

Harrington, Richard. "Jay-Z's Rhymes of Passion." *Washington Post*, January 2, 2000. http://www.washingtonpost.com/wp-srv/WPcap/2000-01/02/058r-010200-idx.html (May 5, 2012).

Jay-Z. *Decoded*. New York: Spiegel & Grau, 2011.

*O, the Oprah Magazine*. "Oprah Talks to Jay-Z." October 2009. http://www.oprah.com/omagazine/Oprah-Interviews-Jay-Z-October-2009-Issue-of-O-Magazine (April 26, 2012).

Pappademas, Alex. "Jay-Z: King." *GQ*, November 2011. http://www.gq.com/moty/2011/jay-z-gq-men-of-the-year-issue (April 27, 2012).

Seliger, Mark. "King of America: From Coachella to the White House, How Jay-Z Runs the Game." *Rolling Stone*, June 24, 2010, 44–47.

Stoute, Steve. *The Tanning of America: How Hip-Hop Created a Culture That Rewrote the Rules of the New Economy*. New York: Gotham Books, 2011.

Taddeo, Lisa. "Jay-Z: It Takes a Harmless, Hand-Built Gangster to Run This Town." *Esquire*, February 2010. http://www.esquire.com/features/people-who-matter-2010/jay-z-business-0210 (May 4, 2012).

Touré. "The Book of Jay." *Rolling Stone*, December 15, 2005.

## FURTHER READING AND WEBSITES

### Books

Barnes, Geoffrey. *Jay-Z*. Broomall, PA: Mason Crest Publishers, 2007.

Golus, Carrie. *Russell Simmons: From Def Jam to Super Rich*. Minneapolis: Twenty-First Century Books, 2012.

———. *Tupac Shakur: Hip-Hop Idol*. Minneapolis: Twenty-First Century Books, 2010.

Heos, Bridget. *Jay-Z*. New York: Rosen Classroom, 2009.

Morgan, Kayla. *Kanye West: Soul-Fired Hip-Hop*. Minneapolis: Twenty-First Century Books, 2012.

Roberts, Russell. *Alicia Keys: Singer, Songwriter, Musician, Actress, and Producer*. Broomhall, PA: Mason Crest Publishers, 2009.

Sacks, Nathan. *American Hip-Hop: Rappers, DJs, and Hard Beats*. Minneapolis: Twenty-First Century Books, 2012.

Waters, Rosa. *Beyoncé*. Broomall, PA: Mason Crest Publishers, 2007.

———. *Hip Hop: A Short History*. Broomall, PA: Mason Crest Publishers, 2007.

### Websites

Beyoncé
> http://www.beyonceonline.com/us/home
> Beyoncé's official website offers videos, photos, and biographical information, plus all the latest news about Beyoncé.

Grammy.com
> http://www.grammy.com
> The Grammys are prestigious music awards given yearly since 1959 by the National Academy of Recording Arts and Sciences. At this site, you can learn about Grammy winners past and present. The site also includes videos, photos, and music news.

Hip-Hop: Beyond Beats and Rhymes
> http://www.pbs.org/independentlens/hiphop/index.htm
> This website explores issues in hip-hop culture including violence and racial identity. The site is a companion piece to a film of the same name. The site includes a timeline of hip-hop history and a glossary of terms.

Rap

http://www.allmusic.com/genre/rap-ma0000002816
This website introduces hip-hop music and its various styles, such as old-school rap and pop-rap. Visitors can click on links to a specific styles, artists, and songs to learn more.

Roc-A-Fella Records

http://www.islanddefjam.com/default.aspx?labelID=75
Visitors to this website can learn about the latest releases and goings-on at Roc-A-Fella Records, the company that Jay-Z founded in 1996.

Roc Nation

http://www.rocnation.com
Roc Nation is Jay-Z's music label and management business. On the website, you can learn about Roc Nation artists such as J. Cole and Willow Smith.

Shawn Carter Scholarship Foundation

http://www.shawncarter.com
Jay-Z's charitable foundation gives scholarship money to deserving students from low-income families. The website offers information on scholarships, an application form, and additional resources for students.

# INDEX

## PHOTO ACKNOWLEDGMENTS

The images in this book are used with the permission of: © Photo by Todd Plitt/USA TODAY, pp. 1, 37, 97; Mike Segar/Reuters/Newscom, p. 3; © Dan MacMedan/USA TODAY, pp. 4, 38, 98; Seth Poppel Yearbook Library, p. 6; © Kevin Kane/WireImage/Getty Images, p. 7; © Robert Deutsch/USA TODAY, pp. 8 (right), 73, 85; Globe Photos/ZumaPress/Newscom, p. 8 (left); ©Anthony Barboza/Archive Photos/Getty Images, p. 9; © Kevin Mazur/AMA2009/WireImage/ Getty Images, pp. 10, 20, 24, 42 (top), 46, 56, 68, 78, 90 (top); © Robert Hanashiro/USA TODAY, pp. 11, 75; © Ebet Roberts/Redferns/Getty Images, p. 12; © Carol Friedman/CORBIS, p. 14; © Peter Keegan/Stringer/Hutlon Archive/Getty Images, p. 16; Tim Grant/Abaca/Newscom, p. 17; © Djamilla Rosa/WireImage for Bragman Nyman Cafarelli/Getty Images, p. 19; © Jim Wilson/USA TODAY, p. 21; © David Corio/Michael Ochs Archives/Getty Images, p. 23; © Tim Loehrke/USA TODAY, p. 25; © Garrett Hubbard/USA TODAY, p. 26; © Raymond Boyd/Michael Ochs Archives/Getty Images, p. 27; © Larry Ford/CORBIS, p. 28; © David Yellen/CORBIS, pp. 29, 41; © Hulton-Deutsch Collection/CORBIS, p. 30; © Johnny Nunez/WireImage/Getty Images, p. 32; © Clarence Davis/NY Daily News Archive via Getty Images, p. 33; © Time & Life Pictures/ Getty Images, p. 35; © Jim McHugh/CORBIS, p. 36; Zhao Yuis/Zuma Press/Newscom, p. 39; © Rick Williams/USA TODAY, p. 40; © Vince Bucci/AFP/Getty Images, p. 42 (bottom); © Ray Tamarra/Getty Images, p. 44 (left); © RJ Capak/WireImage/Getty Images, p. 44 (right); © SGranitz/WireImage/Getty Images, p. 45; © Frank Micelotta/Getty Images, p. 48; © Johnny Nunez/WireImage/Getty Images, p. 49; © KMazur/WireImage/Getty Images, pp. 51, 57; © Joe Stevens/Retna Ltd./CORBIS, p. 53; © Reebok via Getty Images, p. 54; © Adam Rountree/ Stringer/Getty Images, p. 55; © Bob Riha, Jr./USA TODAY, p. 59; AP Photo/John Raoux, p. 60; © Johnny Nunez/WireImage/Getty Images, p. 61; © ROTA/Getty Images, p. 62; Brian Rasic/Rex USA, p. 63; © Evan Eile/USA TODAY, p. 65; © Scott Gries/Getty Images for Universal Music, p. 67; AP Photo/Obed Zilwa, p. 70; Rex USA, p. 71; © Dave M. Benett/Getty Images, p. 74; © Diana Scrimgeour/Redferns/Getty Images, p. 76; © Jim Dyson/Stringer/Getty Images, p. 77; © Jack Gruber/USA TODAY, p. 79; © Matt Rourke/AP/CORBIS, p. 80; © Timothy A. Clary/ AFP/Getty Images, p. 81; © Lee Jaffe/Hutlon Archives/Getty Images, p. 82; © Rick Wilking/ Reuters/CORBIS, p. 83; © H. Darr Beiser/USA TODAY, p. 84; © Photononstop/SuperStock, p. 86; ©Pool./Retna Ltd./CORBIS, p. 88; © Sayre Berman/CORBIS, p. 89; © Handout/USA TODAY, p. 90 (bottom); Zelig Shaul-Ace Pictures/Newscom, p. 92; © Kevin Mazur/WireImage/Getty Images, p. 94.

Front cover: © Jason Kempin/Getty Images for You Tube.

Back cover: © Todd Plit/USA TODAY

Main body text set in USA TODAY Roman Regular 10.5/15.

## ABOUT THE AUTHOR

Stephen G. Gordon was born in Cleveland, Ohio, and graduated from Kent State University. He makes his home in northern New Mexico, where he writes about sports, history, and music.